God Is Not
In the
Thesaurus

God Is Not
In the
Thesaurus

Stories from An
Oklahoma Prison

Bo Don Cox

Forward Movement Publications
Cincinnati, Ohio

*This book is dedicated
to God, Jesus and Grandpa
who share the best seat in the house.*

Table of Contents

Acknowledgements

I'd like to thank Deborah for simply and majestically being my wife, friend and partner; Dad, Mom, Crockett and the rest of the family for not disowning me, even when it would've been understandable; Grandma and my aunts for all the haircuts, handouts and hands-ups; Sue Hinton for the pencil, paper and push; Bill and all his friends for more than I can say and for the coffee, smiles and hugs; Moses Glidden, Jeff Weimer, Horace Stumblingbear, David Darby and countless other quiet giants for showing me how to be a man; Mike Moore for looking at me and seeing a Choctaw; Mike Gibson for getting up every morning whistling and smiling after thirty-plus years in this place; all prisoners and their families everywhere, inside and out; every prison guard who has ever treated a prisoner or his family with kindness, dignity and respect; Mary Barwell for being my friend; and finally, Ted and the gang at Forward Movement for always saying yes.

Finally, I'd like to offer my apologies to all victims of crime, everywhere.

Introduction

For those who want to save their life will lose it, and those who lose their life for my sake and for the sake of the gospel, will save it. —Mark 8:35

Bo Cox was brought up in Coalgate, Oklahoma. His life changed dramatically on the night of July 26, 1986. Other changes followed as Bo lived and prayed and became a new man in an Oklahoma prison.

He began to write, entered a writing contest, won a substantial award. It was then, 1994, that Bo wrote Forward Movement, sent $50.00 of his prize money, told us he had grown up with *Day By Day*. Could he write a month of meditations? The meditations of November, 1995, later republished under the title *Release*, brought a torrent of response.

Bo continues to write from prison. Two short pamphlets, another series of meditations, and now these *Stories From an Oklahoma Prison*. They tell the story of Bo's life, his old life and his new life. They speak of the power of God and the presence of Jesus Christ in the prison where Bo lives. They speak of hope and promise and new life—behind razor wire and prison walls.

Several times I have been present with Bo behind those walls and know, beyond the shadow of a doubt, that Christ is with us and that in all times and all places we are called to be Christ, one to another. The atmosphere of prison is oppressive, smothering. You will feel it in these pages. Even for those of us who fear dying in prison—and many of us will, in a prison of our own making—God is present. Each time I see Bo in prison, sit and talk with him, exchange letters, I am overwhelmed by respect, awe, admiration. Bo and I are as different as can be, but we have everything in common, for we have Christ.

Bo understands and welcomes the Lord Christ, identifies with Christ, is transformed by Christ. Jesus suffered, was broken, died for Bo, who has been transformed. May we all be.

Bo lives in a prison in Oklahoma. Each of our prisons has a different address. We make them for ourselves, and they hold us captive. But that does not mean we live alone, for we are surrounded by the presence and power of God in Christ.

There is a tradition of powerful Christian testimony written from behind prison walls. These stories from an Oklahoma prison are part of that tradition. They offer the promise of new life.

—Edward S. Gleason
Editor

Your Owner's Manual

Finally, beloved, whatever is true, whatever is honorable, whatever is just, whatever is pure, whatever is pleasing, whatever is commendable, if there is any excellence, and if there is anything worthy of praise, think about these things. —Philippians 4:8

Before you begin . . .

These stories are about people. They're about prison. Some are about people in prison. They're about life, including death. Sometimes they're about doing life. I'd be a liar if I said they weren't also about "the system." They're about God. I'm not a theologian. I'm not a spiritual giant. I'm a stumbling student of life. I'm a sinner. I'm a mistake-maker. I'm a young man, trying—sometimes easily, sometimes desperately—to make sense out of my own little slice of existence.

These stories are my perceptions. Nothing—not prison, death, or life—is black and white. Depending on who you are and where you stand, literally and figuratively, you see shades of gray. This book is gray.

Had a young man named Bart Ennis and I not gotten into a fight on the night of July 26, 1986, had I not caused his death, had I not gone to prison, none of this would have been written. There is more than one side to every story. It would be callous to pretend this is different.

When I quit alcohol and other drugs, it was suggested I make amends to the people I had harmed while I was drinking and using drugs. My list was long. To amend is "to improve" or "to better." The harm I did Bart is irreversible, but I'm still alive and so are you, and we're both a part of humanity, and we can try to improve or better our little corner.

These stories, written from my point of view, are in memory of Bart Ennis. Bart, I have something to tell you: *I'm sorry. I wish I could change that night. Please forgive me.*

The following pages contain stories. Nothing less, nothing more. They are yours.

So What?

So the last will be first, and the first last.
—Matthew 20:16

There are reasons not to write: no place to gather thoughts, no thoughts to gather, sometimes the thoughts that gather aren't worth writing. Lately, it's been easy not to write.

An orderly comes in here every day and starts moving all the desks around. My first thought is how in the world can anyone care this much about a job that only pays ten dollars a month? Then I think he might be doing it just to bother me. After all, this is the only relatively quiet time I have to write. I never realized how much noise a guy can make rearranging dust mops in a corner.

When he's not here, someone else is. The other times I have to write are in the middle of a class: a life skill class, taught by the prison staff or college classes, taught by faculty from a junior college. Either way, someone's always making noise or wanting to talk.

"Whatcha doin'?" As if he can't read my body

language. My scowl and hunched shoulders ought to be plain.

If I do manage to get the classroom all to myself, one of the four walls that make up this classroom is also the wall that separates this space from the handball court. What this means for me, the struggling artist, is that I get to blend the sounds of my fingers on the keyboard with the whack, thump, whack of the handball.

Finally, if it's not any of the above, it's me. My attention span, my ability to maintain a sustained thought, is gone. Just the slightest wind—an errant thought, a wandering abstraction—whisks away whatever "magic dust" I gather. It's frustrating and sometimes I wonder if I'm going to be able to continue writing. Lately, I've doubted it.

"Maybe I'm not a writer," I tell myself. "Maybe I should just quit writing."

Before I can settle on that decision, I decide I am a writer. Then I'm not. Then I am.

It can get maddening; especially once you throw in the rest of life. This is my thirteenth year of incarceration; will it stretch into twenty and then disappear into the blurry horizon of forever? Writers should have a better grip on the future.

I'm in love with and married to a beautifully strong and magnificently simple country girl from Kentucky. Being in here while she's out there is a constant challenge and brings new meaning to the word acceptance. Writers should know more about love.

I've come to a place in my journey where I'm not concerned any more with being the loudest or the toughest. Being loud and tough matter in prison, but what matters to me is maturity—growing into the fullness of the person God created me to be. That's important if you want to write. Writers should be grown up.

But I'm full of doubt. Who isn't? And I lack something I had in abundance when I began writing—peace. Back then nothing bothered me. I could sit in the middle of a riot and write a poem. My thoughts weren't jumbled. Orderlies and handball courts were mere pins dropping in an otherwise quiet universe. Today, I'm struggling not to be defined by my environment.

Noise at this prison is a living thing. It permeates the cement walls. Nothing is sacred. There are no quiet places. Everyone believes the only way to rise above the noise is to make more noise. People assume that if you jump up on your own black stallion of sound you'll be impervious to the ordinary din. I can handle the constant rumble. It can shrink into unnoticed background white noise. The spikes are what kill you; someone screaming to be heard or simply to be noisier than the noise; music, existing on an altogether different level, vibrates through yards of steel reinforced concrete and closed heavy metal doors.

Rude is in vogue. It's not accepted etiquette to nod your head or smile politely at a passerby. That will get you nowhere unless you want to be sneered at. What's honored here is icy indifference or stone-cold stares. It's ironic that the feigned aloofness and meanness come from people who are really lonely and scared.

It's not just the guys who live here. It's almost as if madness invites madness. The people who work here aren't exempt from the corruption and perversion that comes with people caging other people. Tom Robbins wrote, "A creature, human or otherwise, that has had its freedom compromised has been degraded. In a subconscious reaction that combines guilt, fear, and contempt, the keepers of the caged—even the observers of the caged—are degraded themselves. The cage is a double degrader. Any bar, whether concrete or intangible, that stands between a living thing and its liberty is a communicable perversity, dangerous to the sanity of everyone concerned." (*Another Roadside Attraction*)

No one walks away from prison without blood on his hands. Whether it be the always-changing/never-changing dilemma of living in prison, the snowballing frustration of not being able to find a truly quiet spot, or the anger that inevitably bubbles up in this hostile environment, this place is beginning to fray me around the edges. Like the gray of winter, it permeates my psyche and my mind, and I start to think I can't write what I believe I've been led to write, which is hope-filled messages proclaiming our risen Lord, and how good ultimately triumphs over bad, and how the sun always comes up even after the darkest nights.

Darkness seems to be winning ninety percent of the time. The nice guys get beat up and have their shoes taken from them. If I do see a light in the dark, it's a flashlight and behind it is some guard who doesn't give a damn about me one way or the other. The noise eats up the quiet, and peace is a memory from another time, another prison.

It makes me angry. If it's true what Jesus said, and it is, that whatever we do in our hearts we actually do, I've hurt quite a few people. I've silenced the noise with violence; I've dealt out cruel justice to the bullies; I've harmed people. In doing so I've realized an ancient truth: "You will not be punished for your anger; you will be punished by your anger."

It's hard, being angry and being Christian. The moments when I am nothing more than anger are instants where God is crowded out of my heart. Anger goes hand-in-hand with self-centeredness. It's true; I can get angry for someone else, but most of the time it's about me, me, me.

There's room in my heart for a little me, but me, me, me leaves no room for God. Me, me, me leaves me blind, and I can't see God in others. Jesus has come to me many times in the eyes, faces, hearts, smiles and tears of the other forgotten and broken men who live here. When I'm consumed with me, I walk right by Jesus on the sidewalk without so much as a grunt. That must make God wince—it does me. For that reason alone, I don't want to be self-centered, or angry. These moments when I am defined by my anger and my self-centered-ness lead to the moments when I wonder whether to write.

What do I have to say? If I can't handle life's challenges without anger and resentment, without sinking into the pit of self, who am I to write about love? When it comes down to life's tests, I'm failing as many as I pass, maybe more. What does *that* qualify me to proclaim?

Everything, that's what. Because as bad as this prison is, as much as evil and fear and darkness seem to be in control, I still believe in good. Every morning I get back up and roll out of my bunk, and when I hit my knees, I have a hope that defies logic. No matter what happened the day before, no matter how many people I killed in my heart, how angry or scared I was, what I felt I'd never forget—it's all undone, and I'm ready to start anew.

Daybreak *always* follows the dark night. Forgiveness *can* follow injury. Renewal springs from exhaustion. Life is after death, yes, but also in the midst of it. The magic comes from trudging that weary road, even when it seems impossible, no matter how much mud you get on your shoes. The magic comes when we manage to step out of our selves long enough to recognize Jesus when we meet him on that road. If that's not what Christianity is all about, then I don't have a clue.

Christianity is about being broken, acknowledging weakness, failing more tests than you pass, struggling and maybe hardly ever getting it right. It's also about winning when last you remembered you were losing. It's about finding our Lord in the most unlikely places and people. It's about a sinner who needs some help. That's me. If that's you, too, then I'm glad I didn't quit writing.

Because, you see it's from out of these unlikely scripts that I've found a life that I wouldn't trade for anything in the world, and I wanted to write and tell you about it.

Bart's Cousin

And the word became flesh . . .   —John 1:14

How are y'all doin'? My name is Bo Cox. I'd like to thank you for coming to prison today. I hope it turns out to be a good experience. You guys look a little up-tight. You okay? Well, let me tell ya somethin': I'm more scared of you than you are of me. So, if I appear a little nervous, please bear with me.

I grew up in a small town in southeastern Oklahoma, not far from where you guys live. As a matter of fact, we used to play ya'll in basketball and baseball. I guess we probably still do, although I wouldn't know; I've been in here for a while.

I was speaking to the Latta, Oklahoma, senior class of 1992. I belong to a group called Straight Talk, and that's what we do, talk straight. We conduct tours of the prison, followed by intense question and answer sessions. Area schools, churches, civic groups come on a regular basis. We share our life experiences with the young and, sometimes, not so young. The way I see it, there's a two-fold advantage. Maybe, we can save some kids from making the same mistakes we've made, and the public has the chance to see that not everyone in prison is a raging, maniacal, developmentally retarded high school dropout and sociopathic loser.

I don't know how it is in Latta today, but in Coalgate, in 1978, smoking weed and drinking were it. Again, I don't know about you guys, but I'm tellin' ya, the first time I got high I fell in love. Man, it felt so good. Those of you with smiles on your faces know what I'm talking about. I thought I had found the way. I was just fifteen and no one, I'm telling you, no one, was going to stop me from getting high. You guys know. I don't expect you to raise your hand or anything, but I do hope you listen. 'Cause, see, y'all, as good as it feels, and believe me— I know how good it feels—there's more.

More than once, I've seen the teachers' shocked expressions as I've admitted to students how good it feels to get high. But honesty is the best policy. Grown-ups didn't shoot straight with me. They told horror stories about the dangers of dope. It was obvious they'd never tried it, and after I did my own research, I found out they'd lied. I didn't go blind, start stealing or foaming at the mouth or put an infant in the dryer.

The truth was I felt good. I was cool, confident. Coolness and confidence are elusive for a fifteen year-old. That's one of the reasons this is a very big thing. Drugs feel good. That's the truth. That's why people do them.

If I don't tell the truth, what's going to happen when someone goes ahead and tries drugs? I become a liar and what I've said becomes a lie. So, it's best to tell the truth. Besides, I don't want them to miss the rest of my story.

You know what? From the time I was fifteen until I graduated, I got loaded every day. Oh sure, on the surface, everything seemed cool. After all, I wasn't stealing to support my habit. Most of my friends were getting high. I hadn't graduated past weed and alcohol so, in my head, I really didn't have a drug problem. Still, there were some people who were concerned about me and what they perceived as a problem. But every time someone approached me, I'd get defensive and point out to them why I didn't have a drug problem. 'If I've got a drug problem, why haven't I been kicked off the team? Why am I still in the Honor Society?' Or, I'd look 'em straight in the eye and say, 'Me? Drugs? Well, yeah, I drink a little, but not all the time. I smoke pot occasionally, who doesn't? I'd never mess with hard drugs.' Does that sound familiar to anyone in this room? Again, you don't have to raise your hand. Just listen. I've got a question for you. Say you were an alcoholic. I'm not saying you are, just imagine that you were. Would you tell anyone?

Hardly anyone would raise a hand on that question. Why?

One reason is those kids have been told one way or another that there is something wrong with being an alcoholic or an addict.

Being an alcoholic or an addict doesn't make one bad, yet we believe it does. So, I ask them to give me their definition of an alcoholic or addict. Usually it's "Someone who drinks all the time." "Someone whose clothes are all wrinkled and they smell." "Someone who steals to support a habit." "Someone who can't hold a job." "Someone with a beer belly." "Someone really skinny."

Sometimes alcoholics or addicts fit stereotypes. More often they don't. That's not the point—what an alcoholic or addict looks like. The point is that we attach a dark cloud of shame to alcoholism and addiction so that even if a person discovers they are one and wants help, most are ashamed to ask for it.

Hey, guys, guess what? I'm an alcoholic. I'm also an addict. And you know what? That's not a bad thing. It simply means that I can't drink or use drugs at all because, once I begin, I can't stop. It doesn't mean I'm a bad person. But you know what? I used to think it did. That was one of the reasons my life got really, really bad before I was desperate enough to look at the possibility of my being an alcoholic and addict. The bottom line? Once I admitted it, I discovered it was nothing to be ashamed of. It doesn't mean that I'm a cheater, liar, thief, loser, drunk or junkie. All it means is that I can't drink or use drugs.

That usually gets their attention. Here is a relatively together-looking guy, in good physical shape, happy, well-groomed, with a glow in his eye, definitely not chemically induced. It feels good to see them look at one another, raise their eyebrows. It changes their perception. Someday, if they ever discover they need help, it may save their life.

How many of you guys play baseball? Basketball? How about you girls? Basketball? Softball? Are any of you in the Honor Society? Would you believe I lettered four years in football, three in basketball and two in baseball? Would you believe that during senior year I was a captain of a football team ranked fifth in the state? I was in the Honor Society. All through high school I went steady with the smartest girl in our school.

What really scares me is that just as people have misconceptions about alcoholism and addiction, others are as ignorant as I once was concerning prisons. I grew up between McAlester and Stringtown—two of Oklahoma's biggest prisons. It was no big deal to drive by the crews of white-shirted, tattooed men on the sides of the highways, as they picked up trash and cut weeds, while the armed guards on horseback, made sure they didn't escape. Although I felt something disturbing, I wouldn't look twice as I drove by the huge, draconian complexes. Just about every highway sported a sign saying: WARNING: HITCHHIKERS MAY BE ESCAPING CONVICTS.

I was used to prisons. I knew a lot of people who worked there; however, I didn't know any of the men who lived there. I knew they must be different from me or any of my friends. I assumed they were men who were born bad, did bad things, and when they turned eighteen were sent to prison.

The biggest mistake young visitors (actually *all* people of *all* ages) can make it is to walk out thinking they're different from me. They're not. Every time I talk to a school group, I look back and can see myself sitting in the back row.

So, guys, I graduated from high school with a formidable drug habit. Now, I didn't know that I was already out of control. I still believed that I could handle

*drugs. And, it wasn't just beer and weed anymore. Nope.
When I started, I'd swore that being an athlete, I'd never
do anything harder than drinking and smoking weed.
By the time I had graduated from high school I'd tried
everything—pills, crank, coke, snorting, shooting; anything that would get me high. There wasn't a drug I
wouldn't try. I tried college. Twice. Dropped out both
times. I tried work. Quit every job I got. Of course, none
of these things was ever my fault. It just happened.*

By this time, a couple years after I'd graduated from
high school, I was in the midst of a full-blown amphetamine addiction. For the next year and a half, I was a
speed junkie. When it all caught up with me and I got in
trouble, I weighed one hundred and thirty-five pounds
and looked like a skeleton.

This never fails to get their attention. Looking at
me, it *is* hard to conceive. Here's this guy, almost two
hundred pounds, healthy as a horse, happy and smiling.
It just doesn't add up. *He* was a junkie? They begin to
pay closer attention. This group was no exception. I
noticed them sitting up in their seats . . . looks of amazement, distaste, pity . . . everything.

I was in trouble, busted with a bunch of my 'friends'
and we all landed in jail. Even though we swore alle-
giance to one another, the minute we landed in jail
everyone started to tell on one another. All the romance
and exciting outlaw stuff went out the window. It was
dog eat dog. Sitting in jail I realized my life was a mess.
But I missed the point, even though I had had an awak-
ening. I decided I had a problem with hard drugs, and I
would have to do what it took to leave them alone. But
stupidly I thought I could still handle drinking and

smoking pot. Those things were okay. Everyone did them, and I'd never gotten in real trouble.

It's not the easiest thing in the world to tell a group of strangers how stupid you were. But it's important for two reasons: first, it's a perfect illustration of the insanity of alcoholism and addiction, and second, I see people nod when I say that hard drugs are dangerous, yet look the other way when it comes to alcohol and marijuana, especially alcohol.

Thinking that alcohol is different, okay, acceptable, is one of the biggest mistakes I made. I want every person who hears me speak, especially those who nod their heads in approval when I tell them how I laid down the "hard stuff" in favor of "just drinking," to know exactly how grave that misconception is.

For the next few months, life was as good as it had ever been for me. It's true: I wasn't strung out on drugs anymore. I even had a job. Even though I drank heavily and smoked pot every day, people, myself included, thought I was getting it together. On July 25, 1996, after a day of driving a dump truck, I got off work and me and a few of my buddies started drinking—just like any other Friday.

If I were the least bit nervous when I began, this is the point my nervousness raises to new heights. My voice quivers, my heart begins to race, I start to sweat. July 26, 1986, isn't easy to live with, and my body protests when I relive it. Every time I tell the story it gets a little easier, but never easy enough.

So after drinking all afternoon, all evening and all night, I found myself on Main Street about two o'clock in the morning. I'm not sure how it all happened, but I know it started when Bart and I started calling each other names. That's right, calling each other names. Pretty stupid. I got out of my truck, and we started to fight. Everyone gathered around, egging us on, hollering, cussing—you know how it is in a fight when everyone is drunk. Before I knew what was happening I'd stopped fighting the first guy and another guy had jumped in. At this stage in the game I realized that I was outnumbered, and I had better get my tail out of there. So, I did. I left.

This should be the end of this story. But it's not because, you see, when I got a few blocks down the street I started thinking about how everyone was going to call me a sissy the next day for leaving the fight and letting those guys run me off. This is an important point. How many of you guys, girls too, when you get in a fight, fight because you're tough? How many of you fight because you're afraid of what people will say if you don't? Let me tell you guys something: I've not once been in a fight where I wasn't scared to death. I'm not just talking about being scared of getting beat up. Thing is, I've always been more scared of what people would think about me if I didn't fight.

You should see the faces on the kids. They understand. There aren't many of them who are ready to raise their hands and say, "Yeah, the only reason I fight is I'm scared everyone will think I'm a sissy if I don't." They don't have to raise their hands and say it. I can see it in their eyes. In the way they drop their heads, look at the floor and shuffle their feet.

So after driving down the road a few blocks, I turned around and went back and called everyone names as I drove by. They all jumped in their cars and followed me out of town. I pulled off on a dirt road and got a baseball bat out of my pickup. I was gonna show them I wasn't scared.

Suddenly I heard hysterical sobbing in the back row. It was a girl I'd noticed staring at me. She had her head buried in her hands, and her small body was being racked by loud, uncontrollable sobs. I couldn't stop watching her. I saw her teacher rush to her side. So did her principal and a best friend. Everyone was watching the little circle around her. I became so distracted I lost track of what I was saying, wound up the story and sat down. I wanted to disappear. I'd had people cry before when I was talking. It's understandable. This is a sad, tragic, story and unsettling. Still, I wondered what had upset her so much.

I looked at her, and when she finally met my gaze, I saw something that scared me. I knew. I knew what she was coming to tell me, what the essence of her message was going to be.

"Bo, that little girl is the cousin of the guy you killed."

I don't have the words to describe what I felt at that moment. Scared is an understatement. Sorry is so inadequate.

"She wants to talk with you."

I was paralyzed. My friends told me later that I turned as white as a sheet. I'd been in prison for six years. I'd slept in the same rooms with men who had murdered, robbed, raped, assaulted. Not once had I been as terrified as I was of this little 17-year-old girl, who simply wanted to sit down and talk.

"Bo, do you want to? You don't have to."

Yes, I did.

All of us—the teacher, the principal, the best friend, Bart's cousin and I—went off to a quiet corner and sat down in a circle. Someone started talking, trying to mediate. All I could do was sit there, head hanging, and wring my hands, trying to muster the courage to raise my head and look the girl in the eye.

After a moment I managed to look up. She said, "I just want you to know that I don't hate you."

"Thank you."

Time was suspended. Everyone else tried to fill the silence. I can't remember what they said. I could hear them, nodded my head, struggled like a drowning person to find some words. I couldn't.

Words weren't necessary. As everyone got up to leave, she smiled. It wasn't a pretty, everything-is-better-now, I'm glad-we-had-this-talk, now-I'm-okay smile, but a smile full of hurt and confusion and forgiveness and love. It must've been difficult to smile that smile, and it must have felt good.

In that tear-streaked smile I began to get a glimpse, literally and figuratively, of God. It's understandable that she could hate me. Yet she didn't. Even though it feels good and even though I want it, I don't feel like I deserve her forgiveness, but there are moments when I am able to accept it and know it.

Somewhere in the middle of all that, there lies an elusive and a very sacred truth: the word *can* become flesh. I know. The word was a petite, brown-eyed, black-haired girl that day. The word was hurt and scared. The word was, and is, alive.

The Old People

Whoever welcomes one such child in my name welcomes me, and whoever welcomes me welcomes not me but the one who sent me.   —Mark 9:37

St. Peter's Episcopal Church smelled like mothballs. I hated it.

Only old people went there. It was like sitting in a retirement home. Besides, I couldn't understand that weird, archaic language. Why did we always have to read the same boring stuff from the same book? The monotony and rote were worse than school.

To make matters worse, across the street was the Baptist Church where the majority of my schoolmates attended. Over there, it seemed, there weren't *any* adults and *no* old people. On their huge front lawn, amid screams of joy and much laughter, hordes of young people played—are you ready for this?—games. That's right. While my senses were being subjected to hard oak pews, dim lights, foreign language and an overwhelming smell of Absorbine Jr., stale cigarette smoke, Sweet Garrett snuff and mothballs, my schoolmates were playing volleyball, softball and tag. God appeared to be

a lot more fun on the other side of the street and, as a young boy, I wondered why I couldn't have been born a Baptist.

During my early teenage years church got better. We got a new priest, Father Bill Winston; let me call him Bill. He had long hair and a beard and in my first theological reflection I wondered if Jesus looked like Father Bill. Not only did Bill represent a kinder, gentler God, he involved me in the services. When I became an acolyte, what we did in the Episcopal Church began to take on a whole new meaning. His teachings started to shine much-needed light on the confusing services and before long I began to appreciate what was going on and developed relationships with older people. Things that had made no sense, like the mysticism of communion and the symbolism of candle light became captivating.

But not as captivating as drugs. The flicker of church candles on the shadowed altar faded in the glow of burning marijuana in the back seats of cars on dark country roads. A sip of wine at Communion with my Lord was lost in endless gulps of liquor and oblivion from life and from my Lord. The seasoned counsel of elders, who loved me enough to tell me the truth even when I didn't want to hear it, gave way to the counsel of well-intentioned, unaware peers, whose best advice was to try anything once, and if it felt good, do it again. I took things a step further, and if it felt good, I overdid it.

Before I began to quit everything else, I quit church. Later I quit basketball. (The coach had it in for me.) I quit college. (I wasn't cut out for it. Everyone there was fake.) I quit every job. (Some unreasonable boss would invariably fire me for no reason.) I even quit obeying laws. (They were unfair.)

The only thing I wouldn't quit was getting high and drinking. This was my new religion. In the forgetfulness of chemicals I found the only peace I knew: peace from myself and from the consequences of the way I was living. It wasn't too long before my marijuana and alcohol habit turned into an anything-that-would-get-me-away-from-the-reality-of-life habit.

I was in that altered, yet familiar, state the night I killed Bart.

Four months later, I was on my way to prison with a life sentence.

I remember the day they brought me to prison. Coming from a small town meant you knew everyone, and everyone knew you. The deputy sheriff who took me to prison was a guy who'd been a few years ahead of me in high school. I knew him and his whole family, and he knew me and mine. Although I'd already been in solitary confinement in the county jail for four months, I still had no idea what to expect. Any given day in our small county jail resembled an episode from the Andy Griffith Show. That is why, when we pulled up to the huge, ominous building surrounded by the double, twelve-foot fences, topped with razor-wire, complete with armed guards at the gate, I got scared. I wanted to reach out and hug the deputy and beg him not to make me get out.

But I didn't. I played it tough. I smiled and joked and acted like I wasn't scared. Looking back, I'm sure that my little act was transparent. We pulled through the big double gates, and I got out, went inside the electronic doors into a new world. Bill took my chains off, told me to take care of myself, turned and left.

"What's your name?" the guard asked without looking at me, although I was looking at him, trying to catch his eye to let him see I was a nice person.

"Bo Cox." I replied.

"I don't need a first name, Cox. Your number is one-five-oh, six-five-six. Remember it."

Another guard came up. "Move along to the next

door. Wait until they call your number. Step inside. No talking. Don't cross the yellow line. Move it."

I tried to smile at him to show him that I would try to get along, but there was no use. He wasn't having any of it, and suddenly I was beginning to get a taste of what my life was going to be like.

Over the next four hours I was stripped, had every orifice in my body probed, my head shaved, my clothes replaced with an orange jumpsuit, was yelled at, crammed into starkly-lit, closet-sized rooms with other jumpsuited men and herded around like cattle until that night, when they finally put me in my own cell. I was in prison.

Another stern-faced guard showed me to my cell, unlocked the door and stepped aside as I walked in. Lying on the bottom of two steel bunks attached to the wall was a man wearing coveralls like mine, the top rolled down around his waist, his torso covered by tattoos. He was reading a paperback. At his side, on the edge of an empty cardboard-box-turned-coffee-table, sat a stained Styrofoam cup full of coffee and a dented Pepsi can with a hand-rolled cigarette sitting on top, trailing smoke to the ceiling. Even though this was a new world, something told me none of this was new to my cellmate. He seemed completely at home.

"Hey, what's up?" he said, as the guard locked the door behind me.

"Hi. How ya doin'?" I nodded. I put my belongings—one thin plastic mattress, a set of dirty-white sheets, one yellowed towel, a plastic covered pillow, a small plastic bag containing my toothpaste, shampoo and soap, and three pairs each of grungy gray boxers, socks and shirts—up on the top bunk—my bunk—and sat down.

"You smoke?" he offered me one.

"Thanks man, I got one," I said and pulled out my cigarettes. I'd already heard about accepting "free" gifts from other prisoners.

"First time in?"

"Yeah."

"What for?"

"First degree murder."

"C'mon, man. Really. You ain't gotta lie. What is it? Drugs? Hot checks?"

"Na, I'm serious, man. First degree murder."

"I can't believe it," he said. "Look at you. First degree murder. Uh-uh, I ain't believin' it. You look like some college kid, 'cept for that shaved head."

He laughed at his little joke, and I managed a smile even though nothing was funny.

We talked. He told me about doing time. What to do. What not to do. As we talked into the night, I found myself feeling a little more comfortable with the place where I was destined to exist. Still, I just didn't want to believe this was happening. I remember going to sleep that first night, praying that when I woke up this would all be a dream.

When I awoke, it was all very real, and, although nothing miraculous had happened during the night to make the nightmare disappear, I did make a huge discovery.

There were drugs here. Before lunch of my second day in prison I had found some weed, bought it with some of the cigarettes I had, and got high. As the potent marijuana began to soothe me, I decided that as long as I could get high I could do prison. I still wanted out, but over the course of the next few years, the drugs worked their magic, and I eventually lost sight of that. All I wanted was to be high. Oh, sure, if you asked me, I'd tell you I wanted out, but in reality I wanted to be high. It got to a point where it didn't matter what it was: weed, homemade beer, crank, heroin, coke, or anything injectable. I even tried paint thinner and drank the alcohol squeezed out of bars of Right Guard deodorant because I wanted to be high. Nothing more. Certainly nothing less.

I'd been living like that for eleven years, four of them in prison, when it finally quit working for me.

There were many factors, but I was acutely aware of three reasons that I needed to lay the chemicals down. I woke up one morning and, seemingly in an instant, it was clear that I was spiritually dead. There was nothing left inside. I just couldn't get high enough anymore to ignore that or the tragic shape of my life. What is more, I realized that as long as I continued to get high I had zero chance of getting out of prison.

I had to try to quit getting high. So I did. Tried. That's all it was at first: a wobbly, fearful step into the scary world of reality.

I remember back in the late seventies and early eighties, when my drug use had just begun, there was a saying: "Drugs are for people who can't handle reality." The counterculture came up with an answer to that: "Reality is for people who can't handle drugs." The truth was, in the beginning days of my sobriety, I didn't know if I could handle either.

Somehow I made it. A week passed. I didn't get high. Then, two weeks; then, a month. Almost before I knew it, I had ninety days under my belt. Ninety days without getting high. I couldn't believe it. All my friends were freaking out. They couldn't understand why. Some of them became paranoid around me, thinking I was going "straight." I'll never forget one old-time convict and dope fiend who cussed me out, saying that I'd "sold out to the man." And, in a way, I felt like I had. My whole identity had been wrapped up in the getting, selling and using of drugs. Without that, I was naked. I was a nobody.

For the first couple of months, the only thing I changed was my using. I simply did what recovering alcoholics and addicts call "white-knuckling"— didn't get high. Everything else was the same. All my friends still used. I still hung out in the cell when everyone else was getting high. I would still buy and re-sell drugs for a small profit. I was still in the mix and something told me that if I didn't change that it wouldn't be long until I was right back where I had started.

Not coincidentally, there happened to be an alcohol and drug treatment program at my prison, and there were people I knew in that program who were actually clean and sober. I knew, beyond question, I needed to get in that program, but there was a nine-month waiting list. I couldn't wait for nine months, and if I started getting high again, I was afraid I'd not be able to stop.

I went and spoke with the director of the program who told me I was accepted, but it would be close to a year before I'd be able to move to the housing unit where the program was located. I remember telling him that

I'd been clean for about three months. Was there any way to move me up on the list? He shook his head and told me he was sorry.

I walked out of his office in a state of desperation. What was I going to do?

Before I got back to my cell, I had an idea.

I knew that the drug program was in part funded by the Episcopal Church. Even though I'd turned my back on church, God and the people of St. Peter's, I wondered if there was a chance they'd help get me accelerated admission into the program. The more I thought about it, the more it seemed plausible. At the very least, it couldn't hurt to ask. All they could do was tell me, "No, you had your chance."

I wrote a letter to St. Peter's in Coalgate saying that I had a drug problem, I needed and wanted help, and it was going to take too long, in my opinion, for me to get that help. I didn't feel that I deserved help, and I was afraid. My plea was simple: *If there is anything, anything at all, that you could do to help me, I need it.*

I mailed the letter and told myself I'd give it at least two more weeks. I didn't expect anything. After all, they were just a poor, small parish in the southeast corner of our state. And who was to say they wouldn't say I'd had my chance? It certainly wasn't their fault I was where I was.

A week later, I got a letter from the senior warden at St. Peter's.

"Dear Bo," it began. *"Enclosed, you'll find a copy of the letter we sent to the Bishop. We hope it helps. You're in our prayers."*

I opened the copy of the letter they'd sent to the

Bishop and began reading. Tears welled in my eyes. They told him about the boy they remembered, the young acolyte with the bright eyes and ready smile. The young man with potential. Me. They told him how I'd left church, and how tragic the following years were, not only to me, but to those who loved me. And, most endearing to me, they told him that what had happened four years ago was a terrible, terrible thing, but, nonetheless, an accident.

That was my first experience with forgiveness. They finished up the letter by telling the Bishop they wanted this young man back and implored him to intervene and, please, help me get into the treatment program.

Later that same day I was called back to the director's office. He looked at me with raised eyebrows, a mildly suspicious smirk on his face. "I don't know what you did," he said. "But whatever it was, it worked."

I began to smile.

"Go back to your unit and pack your stuff. You're moving to the Lifeline Program this afternoon."

The young acolyte isn't young anymore. He's been in a medium-security prison since July 26, 1986. He hasn't picked up a drink or any other drug since April 6, 1990. Somewhere along the way he began a relationship with God. His eyes are once again bright; he's gotten his smile back, and he often dreams of the day he can go back and take Communion with the people who saved his life.

The old people.

The Salvage Man

The very stone which the builders rejected has become the head of the corner.   —Matthew 21:42

It was no different from other mornings in prison. The prisoner woke up, looked at his clock—6:45—and at his still-sleeping cell partner. He lay there a minute, rolled over on his stomach, raised himself to his knees and still in bed said a short prayer: *Dear God, whatever. Thank You.*

He got up, made a cup of instant coffee, walked out on the run and lit a cigarette. He'd started smoking again, and while it bothered him, inhaled deeply and enjoyed it. Reaching into the pocket of his gym shorts, he pulled out his daily meditation booklet. As he'd been doing for a good while, he began reading someone else's words on life. Considering the mess he'd made of his, doing it his way, he figured it didn't hurt to accept some guidance.

When his blurry vision stumbled across the word *salvation* he saw *salvage*. He went back to the first of the sentence and read it again. It plainly said *salvation*, right there in black and white. Why, then, was he still seeing *salvage*?

The first thing that came to mind was Skeeter McAlroy, the old man who'd run the junkyard in his small town. He could see him, plain as day, standing there in his grease-stained coveralls, absentmindedly chewing on a huge wad of tobacco, as its brown juice ran a crooked line from the corner of his mouth down through his old, white beard.

He smiled at himself. It was like him to make these seemingly unrelated jumps between scripture and life. Ever since he'd begun writing, his mom had told him that he was going to have a hard time understanding the Bible because he placed too much importance on language, believing that words had dual meanings and thinking that when something says this, it really means that. She believed that the words in the Bible were simple and sacred and her son's wordsmithing complicated plain instructions and risked the chance of corrupting these mandates. He didn't think so.

He figured that God was the master poet and enjoyed the complexity of language as much as anyone, and he'd long ago decided that God was a lot smarter than he could ever hope to comprehend. Trying to fit God into a human-sized box was silly. And if Jesus could speak in parables, why couldn't we play with words and search to uncover meanings beneath the obvious?

And so he thought of the way that Skeeter had run that junkyard. Skeeter didn't conform to society's standards, beginning with the way he wore his tobacco juice and the way he dressed. Except for the time he saw him at grandpa's funeral, he'd never seen him in anything but baggy grease-stained coveralls. Skeeter mumbled when he talked, partly because of the wad in his mouth, partly because he talked to himself. Skeeter was definitely an oddball and walked to a different beat.

Not only did Skeeter look and act differently, his occupation was a deviation from the norm. He took pride in restoring to beauty what someone else had thrown away. He could even make things better than new. He'd dig through the piles at the city dump, rummaging for worthy objects. How did he choose? What did he look for while he sifted through garbage? Was it a glint of light off an old tarnished lamp? Was it the way the pull cord dangled from the long-dead motor of a rusty lawnmower? Was it the absence of food in an abandoned refrigerator, or the lonely sound of its broken door blown back and forth by an occasional breeze? What was it?

Could Skeeter see the personality in the old oak dresser peeking through layers of peeling paint? Were the giggles of its former owner still ringing from the broken bell dangling from the bicycle with no wheels and a rotting seat? Was that it?

Maybe it was all that and maybe it wasn't. Maybe every piece of worthless junk that Skeeter ever laid his magical eyes on became a potential masterpiece, a work of art. Maybe in the twinkling blue eyes that sat above that dirty beard and mumbling mouth, nothing was beyond repair.

The prisoner blew out a puff of smoke and, leaving one foot in scripture and setting the other one down in real life, he decided that God probably looked a lot like Skeeter. As far as he could see, they had a lot in common.

That gave the prisoner a sense of hope. He'd spent the last thirteen years in one of society's junkyards. For all intents and purposes, he'd been thrown away. But that was okay, for if he had not been thrown away, he would never have known what it was to be salvaged. He knew exactly what those forgotten pieces of junk felt like when Skeeter's gaze settled on them.

He smiled again and told God, and Skeeter, *thank you*.

The House
That Jack Built

"Woe to you Pharisees . . . you neglect justice and the love of God . . . And you experts in the law, woe to you, because you load people down with burdens they can hardly carry, and you yourselves will not lift one finger to help them . . . Woe to you experts in the law, because you have taken away the key to knowledge . . . ." When Jesus left there, the Pharisees and the teachers of the law began to oppose him fiercely.

—Luke 11:42, 46, 52, 53

A guy can't have too many heroes. Michael Jordan comes to mind; he's such an inspiration to millions of young people. When I was a kid, my heroes were my Dad, Mohammed Ali and Dr. J. There was also a time when my heroes were people who pushed the constraints of acceptability; there's still a soft spot in my heart for Jimi Hendrix, Jim Morrison and Janis Joplin. Now I've added some new heroes—John the Baptist, Jesus, Martin Luther King Jr., Ghandi, and Neil Young. That common denominator, radical, is still present. Radical is defined as "departing sharply from the traditional or usual," and when that tradition becomes oppressive and self-righteous, it takes courage to stand against peer pressure and do the right thing. So, while on one hand it may be surprising to learn that one of my heroes is an ex-prison warden, it is also apropos. That man is Jack Cowley.

I arrived at the Joseph Harp Correctional Center in January 1989, after spending three years at another state prison. Harp, as it was affectionately called, was the talk of the prison system. Over there, it was said, they had a warden who *let* you get high. They had so many drugs that the guys selling them were having price wars. Open smoke-ins on the ballfield. Conjugal visits once a month. On and on, the rumors were as wild and numerous as the rumor-mongers.

It certainly appealed to me, a young man in search of a better life through the right mixture of chemicals. When I managed to manipulate my transfer to Harp, I was ecstatic. I was finally going to Nirvana. I was moving to Xanadu!

Upon arrival, I was not disappointed. Drugs were plentiful and cheap. It was like one big hippie commune. Unlike other prisons, where the stress was thick, Harp thrived in an atmosphere of peace. There was a huge ballfield with a half-mile track around it. Trees, grass and flowerbeds abounded, not the red dirt and concrete of other state prisons. Once a month, during summer, we were allowed to have our visits on the ballfield. Every weekend, during regular visits, our family and friends were allowed to bring in food. Even though the conjugal visits were pure fantasy, Harp was even better than what I had heard.

In most prisons, you're lucky to see the warden once a month. At Harp, I saw the main man two or three times the first week. He was out on the prison yard, talking with the men who lived there. He called people by first names. He laughed. He joked. He'd holler across the yard at someone if he wanted to talk with them. It struck me as strange. Who was this guy?

When other guys talked about the warden, they called him Jack. Not Warden. Not Mister. But Jack. Most of the men were stuck in a limited mind set of addiction and immaturity, and, while they were very thankful that Cowley let them "get by" with all the perks of Harp, they viewed him as "weak" for letting us have the things he did. I have to confess to once being a part of that crowd. Sure, I liked it at Harp; it was great, but I did think Jack must be a little touched in the head.

Then I met him.

Once a week, he gave a chalk talk for new arrivals. He told us about a place called the real world. It was a place most of us had forgotten. It was a place where we'd proved we couldn't live. He talked about conventional wisdom and the punitive-based philosophies and other stimulus response fallacies so prevalent in corrections. He even said he knew we thought he was weak for being so nice. He said that was what most of the good old boys who made the laws and ran this state thought too and, were it up to them, we'd be locked in a cell twenty-three hours a day, doing time the way it's seen on TV.

Then he told us about Harp. He believed that if he made this place as much like the real world as possible, then, when we got out, we'd stand an infinitely better chance of being a success, not just a person who'd spent incarceration learning how to "do time" the old fashioned way. He told us that he was met with opposition every step of the way, that most lawmakers and their constituents wanted us punished, not catered to, and couldn't see far enough past that fear to understand his philosophy.

He told us that in the local coffee shops when people talked about prison, it wasn't nice. He said the majority of Oklahoma's public wanted us locked up in dark places, scary places, not places with flowers and trees and smiles. They wanted us in "real" prisons, not the "country club" Cowley was permitting. They wanted us to be sorry we were here, and they figured, unless it was pure misery, we'd never reach that state of penitence.

Jack Cowley took exception. He said the only thing we were going to learn in prisons like that, was how to live in prisons like that; and that wasn't going to help us at all when we got out and tried to live in the real world. Even underneath my constant marijuana haze and the double vision of weekly amphetamine use, it made sense.

It took a while but in that fertile atmosphere I sobered up. Crazy. I'd come to a place where the warden allowed more freedom and more chances for wrong choices, and I started making right choices. Right there in the middle of the land of milk and honey, I decided I was going to have to try and live without milk and honey.

So, I took a scary step into the world of "normal." I

wanted to get out as much as the next guy, and it appeared that this place, under Jack's tutelage, was geared toward that end. Not only that, but after I got some sobriety under my belt, it gradually dawned on me that it was actually easier to live without the headaches, heartaches and other consequences of active addiction.

There's a saying in recovery circles: "Keep coming back . . . it gets better . . . then it gets worse . . . then it gets real . . . then it gets different . . . then it gets real different." That pretty much describes the last seven-plus years of my life.

After about two years of sobriety, I was given an early parole hearing. It was a disaster. Murphy's Law was in effect. One parole board member was familiar with the circumstances of my case, and he believed I had received an unusually harsh sentence. He was responsible for my early hearing and assured my family that the board would take a serious look at rectifying the situation. Then a death occured in his family the week of the hearing, and he was abscnt. This left me in front of the other four members without their colleague's backing and with no idea why I was there.

I got one vote, from the oldest, most conservative man on the parole board, the hardest vote. Even though I was devastated, I marveled at the fact that this ultra-conservative had voted for me. It was later that I learned he'd contacted Jack and asked him about prisoner number 150656. Jack had spoken up for me.

Later that week, I got a handwritten note in the mail from Jack. (I still carry it in my address book.) It read: *Bo, Ain't life a bitch at times? I know that you will be*

fine. Handling disappointment is what builds charac-
ter, etc., etc., etc. I know it still hurts. I am sorry for
that. Now pick yourself up and show the world that qual-
ity of life comes from within. As long as there is a breath
in you, there is hope . . . Don't worry, your folks will be
fine too. God bless, JC.

I did manage to pick myself up and, even though I still wanted out, I began to see that the true freedom I'd always been looking for in drugs, and even in release, was inside me. With that spark of truth, I began a new and improved relationship with God. And with Cowley.

This was about the same time that a friend of mine suggested that I write an article for our prison magazine, *Concepts,* and I began to write. Since Jack was directly responsible for the content of our magazine, this involved a working relationship with him. Under his guidance, *Concepts* grew from a stapled, mimeographed flier circulated around the yard into a national award-winning publication boasting a mailing list of over five-hundred. *Concepts* writers won state and national awards.

I won a first place award in the Oklahoma Chapter of The Society of Professional Journalists annual competition, and Jack arranged for me to attend the award banquet. Not only did he allow me to go, I went without the restraints required by the Department of Corrections. It was one of the proudest moments of my life. I felt like a normal person as I sat at my table with a few members of my family and professional journalists from across the state. When they called my name and I walked to the podium to receive my plaque and certificate, I was so grateful, not only because of my success, but

because I was being treated like a person.

   This success of our magazine brought conflict. The Department of Corrections was extremely sensitive. As long as we were a small-time yard rag, we weren't a threat to "the ways things were." But the minute we achieved some renown, we made people nervous. Again, Jack's far-sighted philosophy went to work. He told us to continue the good work. I once overheard him ask one of his superiors if they would rather have us writing about our grievances or throwing rocks through windows as they did at other prisons. Jack fought for us, and I think that was when I really began to see that this man practiced what he preached to the men that lived at his prison.

It was about this time he came up with a ludicrous and far-fetched idea. He wanted to make the whole prison a drug-free environment! That wasn't nearly as unbelievable as the way hc proposed it could happen. He suggested that we, the men who lived here, would be the deciding factor in the success of failure or this goal. Everyone, staff and prisoners alike, thought he was crazy. Prison is not a place for sticking your nose into anyone else's business, and Cowley was insisting that everyone get involved.

At first I resisted. Even though by then I was an outspoken advocate of sobriety and would give my time freely to those who asked, I didn't see it as my job to tell some guy that didn't want to stop that he shouldn't get high anymore. I'd had people doing that to me ever since I'd started getting high and I knew firsthand how futile those efforts had been with me. Not only that, they were dangerous.

Up until that point, Jack Cowley had gained much more than my respect. Without him, this prison wouldn't have had a substance abuse treatment program. Without him, this prison wouldn't have led the state in the number of outside volunteers who came inside and made such tremendous impacts on our lives. Without him, nine prisoners wouldn't have been certified in Reality Therapy and wouldn't have been doing counseling work with our peers. Without him, this would've been just another prison where people "did their time" and were warehoused until they got out. Without him, you wouldn't be reading this because this book never would've been written.

Still, like everyone else, I thought he'd lost his marbles, until I saw him in action outside of prison. The speakout group I was involved in could travel. We were invited to area schools, churches and other civic centers to share our experience, strength and hope with others, namely youth. It was about that time that Jack made a couple of trips with us, and we shared the microphone.

We went to a church in Ardmore, Oklahoma, and I listened as Jack fielded questions. It was clear that, even in church, people were more concerned about punishment than they were forgiveness and reconciliation. I was impressed because he told them the same thing he'd been telling us—anyone could lock someone up, but the key to rehabilitation is grounded in love. He urged them to remember what Jesus said about how to treat those in prison.

The next stop was a parent-teacher conference in Noble. Here Cowley told an auditorium full of people that unless they got actively involved in their own neighborhoods, and in their neighbors' lives, then we wouldn't be able to build enough prisons. He told them that the crime problem began in society and not in prison, and that simply building more prisons to battle crime was like backing ambulances up at the bottom of a cliff to pick up the people who fall as opposed to putting a fence at the edge of that cliff.

HBO did a special on our nations' prisons and filmed

a large part of it right here in Oklahoma. Jack became my hero when he looked into the camera and told the nation that prisons—the way they were currently being operated—were set up to fail. He told people that if prisons ever became successful, they would insure their own extinction. Corrections was becoming too big an industry—too many people were basing their careers on our failures—for the system to let that happen.

After that, instead of a far-fetched dreamer, I saw a visionary, quite like an angry young Jesus overturning tables in a temple where the original purpose had been corrupted.

And, like Jesus, Cowley was attacked. Fired. Officially, they called it a reassignment. In reality it was the first step toward putting him out to pasture.

I was mad. He was selling out, I believed. The department was transferring him to the Oklahoma State Reformatory, a hotbed of trouble. They were trying to paint the move as if it were being done so he could work his magic there. On the day he left, I asked him if that was really the case, and the look in his eyes, coupled with his silence, confirmed my belief.

Once at OSR, he began to make huge changes, trying to implement his philosophy at a place where they were truly still stuck in the Dark Ages. It was disastrous. OSR was infamous for it's protective custody units—places where men who had informed on other men were housed because they were afraid for their safety. Jack did away with that system and told people that they were going to have to be accountable for their own actions: you get in trouble, face the heat, don't tell on someone else and expect him to protect you.

As he'd done at Harp, he opened the prison up and gave people chances to make right decisions. At Harp he hadn't begun his move until he had the full support of his staff. At OSR he didn't have the time for that luxury. Since OSR had been stuck so long in the dark ages, it was too big a jump for staff and prisoners and wrong decisions prevailed. The same philosophy that had worked magic at Harp and gave many a man his life back, ended in two murders and two escapes. Those events ended Jack's career and marked the end of a disappointing short-lived era. The house that Jack built was bulldozed away.

But Jack built something that can't be removed. He built people and in this person, he built hope.

A guy can't have too many heroes.

♪ilent Night

Then an angel of the Lord stood before them, and the glory of the Lord shone around them, and they were terrified. But the angel said to them, "Do not be afraid; for see—I am bringing you good news of great joy for all the people . . ." —Luke 2:9, 10

Christmas. I've got a friend who tells me he dreads this time of year. He says he gets angry when he hears all those Christmas songs. I don't understand. I wish I could feel the same chills run up my spine when I hear those songs in July as I do when I hear them this time of year. I wish the free-giving spirit that seems to prevail during this season would stay with me year-round, not to mention those blessings that come with being a prolific giver. Above all, I wish it were always this easy to love.

Of course it hasn't always been this way. Once Christmas was pure: the thrill of waking up at three or four in the morning to run into the living room to see if Santa had really eaten all the cookies, the innocent joy as my little brother's face lit up on his first few

Christmases. He was so happy in his blissful ignorance of the future. I suppose we all were.

My girlfriend came to our house the Christmas I was in the ninth grade. She was the love of my life, our relationship dating back to the seventh grade. We crept upstairs, where we lay on the floor and kissed. I was the happiest boy in the world that Christmas.

Dad was in rare form too. The last few years I'd noticed a difference in Dad. Something was eating him up and all the whiskey in the world couldn't hide his haunted look as Christmas rolled around. The stranger who'd been visiting these last few years wasn't my dad. This night was different. Somehow, I think he knew how important it was for me to impress Patty, and he didn't let me down.

After that year, Christmas became hell. Booze, drugs and a broken family took its toll on me and my Christmas spirit, and it wasn't long before I found a way to deal with life, especially during this emotional and turbulent time of the year. Life, especially the holidays, was a time to party. Staying completely numb throughout was the only way to beat the Christmas blues and that was how I spent the next twelve years, and all the Christmases too.

In 1990 something changed. In April, after four years in the penitentiary, I'd made a tentative decision to try to get by without getting high. It was relatively easy, mostly because I was tired of the misery that goes along with being out of control of one's life. I was on what recovering alcoholics and addicts call the "pink cloud" stage of recovery—you think now that you've put the chemicals down life is a bowl of cherries. As happy as I was, the closer it came to Christmas, the more I felt uncomfortable about it. I couldn't put my finger on it, but I knew I was definitely bothered by the impending holiday.

Fortunately, I was around a number of caring people who were also trying to experience a sober Christmas. At first I tried to hide in my cell and not let everyone see the tears welling up every time I'd hear a Christmas song—not only on TV, but for 18 hours a day on the loudspeakers across the prison compound. I couldn't go anywhere the days before Christmas without crying. I hid it pretty well. By the time Christmas Day actually rolled around, none of my friends knew what was going on inside me. I was scared. There was this enormous amount of emotion building up ready to burst, and I thought there was something wrong with me.

Christmas night, after hiding in my cell all day, I was persuaded to attend a meeting of alcoholics and addicts. I'd been going to these meetings religiously up until then, but that night I wanted to be alone. I was afraid. I was terrified. The powerful passions boiling inside me were too much. I had to be the only person in the world this scared, and I was embarrassed to let anyone know how much I wanted to cry, how much I felt like a twelve-year-old boy instead of a twenty-seven-year-old man who had spent four years in prison and felt like he had to be tough.

As I sat through the meeting, I continued to suppress the rising wave inside me. I'd look around the room, and as I listened to others talk about how they were handling Christmas without staying loaded and numb, I began to realize this wasn't a bed of roses for anyone.

People were telling how they'd been wondering all day what their families were doing on the outside and if they were missed as much as they were missing. I discovered that a lot of us really had suppressed the spirit of Christmas during our using and drinking days and were now feeling overwhelmed with the power of that spirit. I wasn't the only one who was afraid!

As the meeting drew to a close a man named Moses asked if we'd all care to join hands, turn off the lights, and sing a song. Hesitantly, the words to "Silent Night" began to fill the dark prison chow hall. In an instant, the song took on a life of its own. It came alive. A bunch of ex-drunks and ex-junkies, thieves, murderers, rapists—society's outcasts—were singing like their lives depended on it. And they did. Suddenly, I felt a presence in the room. Someone, or something, was in the room with us, and it was powerful. Warmth flowed from the top of my head down to the bottom of my feet. As the tears rolled down my cheeks, I knew I'd just met God and he'd shown me what Christmas was all about. As the song ended and the lights came back on, I looked around the room at all the red eyes and glowing faces, and I knew they knew. I wasn't afraid anymore.

This Christmas, if you're feeling afraid, depressed, or if you just need to know you're not alone, hum a few bars of "Silent Night" and I promise you somewhere in an Oklahoma prison there will be a group of people singing with you. We'll be together in the truest sense of the word.

The angel was right. Don't be afraid. There *is* great joy coming.

Gary

Let the little children come to me; do not stop them; for it is to such as these that the kingdom of God belongs.

—Mark 10:14

"Ow id u det yor air to cuwl lie dat?"

I really didn't understand what he'd just said until he reached out with his hand and felt my hair. Then I realized he was asking me "How did you get your hair to curl like that."

"It just does that," I told him.

"Oh."

We talked some more. His name was Gary. He wanted to know where I grew up. When I told him, he wanted to know where Coalgate was. That's a typical response for anyone not from rural southeastern Oklahoma.

I asked him how much time he was doing.

"Seh-uhn yeaws."

He asked me how much time I was doing and made a face when I told him. "I'll trade you." I smiled when I said it.

"Oh no." He smiled back. Seven years apparently was enough for him.

So began our friendship.

After that, every time I'd see him on the yard, he'd smile and say, "Ay Bo."

I'd ask him how he was doing. "Oh, pwetty dood."

Gary's face glows with a joy not often seen in prison. Despite his most obvious difficulty, he is enviably uncomplicated, unencumbered.

So why is he in prison? I don't know. From what I know about God, it really doesn't matter. Forgiveness is a mighty big thing.

You know how, when you look in the eyes of "special" people, you see that glow? Gary's got it. Sometimes I wonder if they're not already in the kingdom of heaven. Looking in Gary's eyes, it's plain to see the kingdom isn't far off.

One day I was in front of the visiting room waiting for a visit and he walked up.

"Duz Yilkashn hab a bizet?" he asked the officer.

"Uh, no," the guard replied without checking the list.

"Does Wilkerson have a visit?" I asked the guard. I knew he hadn't understood him.

"Oh. Not yet," he replied, after checking the list.

It makes me wonder. I know people who are diffcrent make the rest of us uncomfortable. Has Gary been told "no" all his life—simply because he has a severe speech impediment and people want to get rid of him rather than communicate with him? Is that why he's so docile? Is he so used to being told "no" that he thinks it's the answer to every question?

I've got some questions: How many times during his trial did Gary ask a question and the judge or lawyer not understand, and instcad of asking him to repeat himself, just said "no"? Is that why Gary's in prison? How many more are there like Gary?

It's sad. We've got a prison overcrowding problem in Oklahoma and Gary is taking up a bed.

Brothers

Am I my brother's keeper?　　　　　　　—Genesis 4:9

"Dad, I just want to know one thing: Who does my brother think he is, calling me collect and telling me how to live my life?" My brother was speaking.

I had telephoned him at his new apartment. It was the first time since I'd been in prison I'd been able to call him at a place he called his own. He'd graduated from college that spring and by summer had landed a good job outside Beaumont, Texas. For most people this is nothing more than simple progression, but for my twenty-nine-year-old brother this was a miracle. He was such an innocent as a child. I guess we all are. Maybe it was because he was a blond-headed, blue-eyed baby in a family of black hair and dark brown eyes. My earliest memories of him are of those sparkling eyes shining like blue gems as I'd push him down the hallway in our clothes hamper with wheels. He'd yell at the top of his lungs, and I felt like the best big brother in the world. I could see the trust in those eyes. I was his hero. That felt good.

As brothers sometimes do, I abused that trust. I'd trick him into doing things. It was easy; he trusted me implicitly. I could convince him of anything. As boys, this wasn't a bad thing, until everything changed.

As a teen-ager, full of rebellion, I began to violate sibling love in ways that haunt me. I knew he was scared of the dark, and yet I'd force him to get off my motorcycle to open the gate across the road leading to our house. The road was actually an abandoned rail-road bed that wound through about two hundred yards of old oak and elm trees. The railroad bed had been there so long the trees grew together overhead. The result was a two-hundred yard lane, completely black, devoid of light even on the brightest moonlit night. Ichabod Crane would have trembled in his boots had he been forced to travel down our road at night. My brother was terrified by it.

"Bo, you're not going to take off and leave me, are you?" he'd ask, looking at me with those trusting blue eyes. "Promise me you won't."

"I won't. I swear." It's no fun looking back and realizing I'd become a liar. He'd get off the back of my motorcycle, and as soon as he'd unlock the wide iron gate, I'd gun my motorcycle and speed past, leaving him in the dark. It hurts remembering the sound of him screaming my name. I could hear it over the whine of my motorcycle's engine.

I'd get to the end of the lane where it turned off the railroad bed and crossed through a wide-open pasture, and sitting in the relative brightness of the moon and stars I'd kill the engine and wait on him to come running out of the darkness. He'd be out of breath and

trembling, crying because he couldn't believe I'd done it again.

I guess it was some sort of lame justification, but as added cruelty I'd scold him for being scared of the dark. "See? there's nothing out there. You've got to quit being scared of nothing. Quit being a baby. You're nine years old. You're not supposed to be scared of the dark." He'd wipe his tears and tell me, "I know, but I don't like it when you do that."

How anybody could continue to trust someone after that, I don't know. But he did. I remained my brother's hero. For awhile.

I began getting high when I was about fifteen. At first it was something I hid. Eventually, though, I no longer cared about hiding it. In fact, I became an outspoken advocate of smoking weed. I believed whole-heatedly in its benefits, and I was convinced with a never-before-experienced-conviction that all the grown-up "experts" on the subject were oppressive brainwashers, trying to keep us from having what I considered was my right: fun.

Crockett, my brother, was about eleven when I first started getting him high. During the summer my friends and I would gather at my house while Mom was at work. We would go up to my room and smoke weed and listen to records. I was in charge of watching my brother, and he'd be there with us. There was confusion in his eyes the first time he actually saw us pull out some pot and begin rolling it up, getting ready to smoke it.

In my extreme self-centeredness and impaired perception, I tried not to notice. Here was an eleven-year old boy, fresh out of a divorce that had ripped apart the safety net of his world, and his older brother, the only stability left in his life, was preparing to do something illegal, forbidden and wrong. Looking back, I can only imagine the confusion I created.

Yet in the perverted view I had, it seemed perfectly natural to "turn my brother on." Getting high felt better than anything I'd experienced, and I actually thought I was doing him a favor. There was the added benefit of course, that if he got high too, he couldn't very well tell Mom.

So, I took his hand and led him down a road much darker than the one he feared a few years earlier. It is no consolation I went down it with him. Only haunting guilt.

I began to fade as a hero. Getting high wasn't something he wanted to do; he only did so because his big brother was forcing him to. Later that summer when Mom came crashing through the bedroom door and found us stoned, she stopped trusting me with his care. He was granted some much-needed space away from my corrupting influence. Given his own room in which to think and make decisions, he decided not to follow me—not for a while.

I changed from a good student to someone who did only what he had to do to get by, from a young man who had sworn never to do drugs to a full-blown weed head, who didn't like people unless they were of a like mind.

My brother was not of a like mind.

I wonder how much it hurt, watching his hero fade. I wonder what thoughts went through his mind when he saw me come home not once, but twice, failing to finish my first semester of college. I wonder what it felt like to be the brother of a guy who'd once been a captain on the best football team our town had seen in years and now was a bum, living at home with his mom, spending his days drinking and partying, unable to hold a job, continually in trouble, and consistently getting worse.

Crockett had just started high school when I first realized he was embarrassed by me, embarrassed to be my brother. The first time I realized it was at one of his baseball games.

He had the sweetest swing. As a freshman his batting average was the best in the state. Watching him bat, you realized you were watching something special. It was so natural. He could hit spraying line drives wherever he chose, or he could hit with power, sending mammoth shots deep over the fence. Rarely did he strike out. My friends and I, the same group who had introduced him to drugs, would get together and watch his games. Sitting on the hoods of our cars, stereos blaring, out along the outfield fence, away from everyone else, we'd drink and smoke without hassle.

After the game I'd stumble over and try to talk to him. He didn't ignore me, but I knew he was ashamed of me. I was a drunk, a doper, a failure.

We drifted apart. Even though we still lived in the same house, we barely talked. Then something happened.

Crockett was fifteen when he began to drink. Then he began to smoke marijuana. The fact he'd changed his views on "stuff" gave us a commonality. I once again became a sort of hero. When he and his friends wanted to drink I could get beer for them. When they wanted some dope, they came to me. But I was still an embarrassment. Four years out of high school, my friends and I hung out at parties with high school kids. We were useful to buy beer and provide drugs, but pitiful when, after drinking all day, we'd show up at one of their parties stumbling around, making fools of ourselves.

For awhile I thought my brother was a casual user. Even after I sat on the side of that same railroad bed he once feared, holding his head in my lap as he threw-up all night after drinking, I still failed to acknowledge a problem. In a twisted, sad way, that was the most tender moment we'd shared since I had started alcohol and drugs.

Not long after that night, I went to jail for killing one of his friends after a party.

Crockett went to college on a baseball scholarship.

I'll never forget the first letter I got from him. He told me not to worry, that he was going to be okay. He was playing ball, he said, and he'd come see me as soon as he could. He signed it, "Love, your brother, Crockett."

I was still in the county jail, awaiting trial, when he got arrested for selling amphetamines to an undercover cop.

Consumed with my own predicament, I was still devastated and felt I was to blame for Crockett's problems. My stay in the county jail was the longest period of sobriety since I'd started drugs. In a desperate bargain with God, I promised that if he would get me out of this one, I'd never use again. I'd once again be my brother's hero. I'd get my life together so I could help him with his. I spent those last few weeks before my trial believing God had said, "Okay, you've got a deal."

When I was convicted and sent to prison, I turned my back on God. And went back to what I knew best.

Crockett got out of his first scrape with the law and went to another college to play ball. But that didn't last. The same insidious obsession that had ruled my life for so long became his. Within a span of three years he had been kicked off teams for drinking and drug-related occurrences at each of three colleges. He dropped out and began the same life he'd seen me lead.

Then I sobered up. Given my own history I would not presume to detail the depths his addiction took him to. I got a firsthand taste of what it feels like to see someone you love deeply destroy himself.

I understand what it feels like knowing in your heart what you are doing is self-destructive, but doing it anyway. I also know there is not a great deal anyone can do for a person once they reach that stage except to let it run its course and be there when they're ready to ask for help.

Some people find sobriety after one bad experience, some have to spend a number of years in the sewer of addiction, some have to come to prison, and, finally, some die because they never find it. While I knew Crockett needed to hit bottom before he could begin to crawl back up, I desperately hoped that his bottom wouldn't rise up to meet him in some cell, or worse, a casket. I hoped it wouldn't take Crockett long to reach a level of self-honesty required to admit he couldn't use any alcohol or drugs, and it didn't.

In the middle of another bout with amphetamines, he went to Mom, who helped him get into a treatment center. Even though he left that one prematurely, he was on his way—finally. That was over two years ago.

Crockett doesn't subscribe to the same beliefs I do, but what he's found works for him, and we are once again on the same path. This time it's well-lighted and headed in a better direction. It's been a long time since we've simply been able to be the brothers we once were, a long time since I've been able to look into his eyes and not see confusion and hurt. Even though a prison fence stands between us, even though we're miles apart as individuals, we're brothers once again. It feels good to be a brother again and to have mine back.

So even when he's griping to Dad about my advice, I know he's as grateful as I am. And even though he may not admit it, he once again looks up to me. It's very humbling to be looked up to when you've done so much not to deserve it. It's just like when we were kids. Except for one thing.

I'll never again leave him alone in the dark.

Friends and
Ice Cream

*I tell you that out of these stones God can raise up
children for Abraham.* —Matthew 3:9

On a Saturday night in February 1997, six of us were
eating ice cream in a tiny prison cell. By the half-gallon
we ate rocky road, triple chocolate, bowls and bowls—
laughing and cutting up like boys at a slumber party.

Except we're not boys. Four are serving time for
killing, one for assault, one for manufacturing and selling drugs. Our sentences add up to two life sentences
and over a hundred years. So far we've been in prison a
total of forty-three years. If you judge us from the
descriptions filed in our records, you wouldn't want us
in *your* neighborhood. We're hard-core, long-term,
violent offenders.

Some introductions:

Fifteen years ago, Jerry killed a man in a drunken
brawl. That's not the reason he's my hero. He's
my hero because he's taught me that happiness,
contentment and joy come from inside, not outside.

I look up to him and respect him. When I'm hurting, I go to him. He's a person in whom I see peace. He's been a lot of things in his life: drifter, drunk, doper, down-and-out. Today, after five years of sobriety, he's a computer programmer, leader, helper and hero. He's found a design for living that works and his life is all about sharing that with others. He's my John the Baptist.

Skip's my cell partner. Before he started drinking, he was an avid and accomplished athlete, a good scholar, an all-around good kid. Once he started drinking, it progressed rapidly, and the years turned into a blur. He was a freshman at Oklahoma State University, five years ago, when he shot and killed one of his best friends during an alcoholic blackout. For most people that sounds like a cop-out, a way to avoid owning responsibility for one's actions. To someone who knows what it's like to drink when you swear you're not going to and then, once you start, not to remember anything after the first couple of drinks, it's reality. Many a night Skip and I sit up until the wee hours, and I listen to the young man try to make sense out of his life. It's been a blessing to watch him uncover the forgiveness for himself that he needs. In the process, he's taught me to find a balance between accepting responsibility for my own actions and at the same time not letting my past prevent me from claiming my future.

If I had a penny for each time David has told me how much his friends mean to him, I could buy my way out of prison. Drugs and alcohol were a way of life for David at a very early age. A simple progression led to his arrest and conviction for drug sales. He's never known anything else, until he came here. He's the father of two little boys and when he talks about them, tears come. You may well say, "if those boys were so important to him he wouldn't have come to prison." There is truth in that statement. But when addiction is part of the equation, then logic, the "ought-to's" and "should-have's" go out the window. When David tells me how special we are to him, I wonder if he knows how special he is to us. He's a rock.

Richard killed someone in a car wreck. He was messed up by pills and booze when it happened. But that's not what I think about when I think about Richard. I think about a summer evening two years ago. A group of us were sitting around talking about life, sobriety, God, prison, and an assortment of other subjects. Richard had recently arrived from another prison. Like me, he'd spent his first years in prison still looking for the answer in a joint, pill or shot. He was sitting away from the group, on the outer edge, not really belonging. When he spoke, I got goosebumps. There was no denying the urgency or sincerity in his voice.

"I gotta clean up," he said. "I'm thirty-four years old, and I've failed at everything I've tried. It's gotta be answered prayer or something that I'm at this prison with you guys because I think this is my last chance, and I can't fail this time." He'll celebrate two years of sobriety this summer, and we'll eat ice cream at his birthday party, too.

And that's what we were doing in that cell: having a birthday party.

Daniel had been clean and sober one year. This guy had been in and out of treatment centers for a decade. Most of the people he knew, including himself, had written him off as a hopeless case. He just couldn't stay sober. He'd get a few months under his belt and, wham, find himself loaded and wondering how that happened. After more than a few years of that, he had come to believe that he probably couldn't do it. The first time I met him I wondered. I don't wonder any more. In the last year, God has spoken volumes about life, hope, faith, love and perseverance through Daniel. I've listened and so has everyone else he knows.

These are my friends. They're the best friends I've ever had, and I'm a better friend because of them. We've cried and laughed together, learned together, sobered up together, grown up together. Most important, we've learned to love together. It's an amazing story, and sometimes I still can't believe it took place right here—in prison.

There we all were, eating ice cream, celebrating Daniel's birthday when, suddenly, David looked up from his bowl of ice cream and, with a quiver in his voice, said, "You know something? This is a miracle."

The Winner—a letter to a grandmother

Hear, my child, and accept my words that the years of your life may be many. I have taught you the way of wisdom; I have led you in the paths of uprightness. When you walk, your step will not be hampered; and if you run, you will not stumble. —Proverbs 4:10-12

You used to let me win.

I wasn't yet ten, in the latter part of the same decade when President Kennedy was shot, the Beatles came to America, Joe Namath was quarterback of the Jets, and there was a war in a place called Vietnam. I doubt you could look at me then and tell that someday I'd end up in prison.

Today I'm past thirty, lots of people have been shot, including one of the Beatles. No one knows the name of the Jets' quarterback, and there's a war in your home town every night on the news. I wonder if you can look at me and tell that I've spent the last thirteen years in prison?

When I decided to write this, I had to comb through all that I remembered about you, Grandma, besides the races we ran when I was a child. I can remember the leaves in your yard. They were shoe-top deep, an impairment to a kid who couldn't yet step high enough to glide when he ran, mostly because his knees weren't that far from the tops of his feet.

I remember the stone-lined ditch that ran in front of your house and the cement bridge over it, leading to your front gate. That was a magical world for me until I got too old to let my imagination make it a foxhole in yet another Apache/cavalry war, the Grand Canyon, or the Amazon River.

I remember going to Ray's Diner, where you worked. You'd treat me like a king and let me order anything I wanted. You made me feel important when I went to Ray's.

I remember walks with you. We'd go downtown. On the way we'd pass the Mamie Johnson Elementary School, and I'd wonder what it'd be like to go to school in a strange town. And I remember once we'd get to Main Street you'd show me off to the people you knew. Maybe that's the thing I remember most about you: you made me feel like I was your favorite.

When I got older I started pulling away from family, being rebellious, trying to "find myself," all that madness. It must have been pretty hard to approve of the things I was doing; but you never failed to let me know how much I was loved every time you saw me.

That's got a lot to do with writing this. I haven't seen you in almost ten years and, barring a miracle,

I won't again. That's a sad thought. It almost makes me want to pout and feel sorry for myself. But I won't. If my life had not taken this route, I wouldn't be the man I am today. Even though you'd love me regardless of the kind of person I turned out to be, it would feel good to be someone you could be proud of. Just like when I was a kid, we could walk downtown and you could still show me off, make me feel like your favorite.

I asked Mom and Dad what they remembered about you.

Dad looked at me and, before he said a word, his eyes told the story: admiration. He talked a lot about you and, even though you two aren't son-in-law and mother-in-law anymore, there was a light in his eyes that's not there unless he's talking about someone special. There's one thing he said that keeps running through my head: "She'd give you her last dollar if you needed it."

Mom told me a story about you I'd never heard. On a Thanksgiving Day once, two policemen stopped in Ray's Diner with a prisoner they were transporting. The two cops ordered themselves something to eat, ignoring the man they were holding captive. You saw this and told the cook to fix him a plate, and you served it to him. About the time they finished eating a call came over their radio saying the man they had in chains was the wrong man.

Mom told me you re-told her this story just a few weeks ago, that it was something you said you'd never forgotten. She told me you said you'll always remember the look on that man's face when they told him he could go free. I'm sure you can understand, given my present circumstances, how that story grabs me. If you'd never been my hero, you are now.

You know, Nanny, I'm sure I've told you "I love you" a thousand times. But I never realized how much until I heard that story.

Let me see: you let me be a winner, you treated me like your favorite, you'd give your last dollar to someone in need, you fed prisoners *and you rejoiced when they were set free,* you loved me even when I was acting unlovable. Those are the same things Jesus did. I hope when I get to be your age, someone can look back at my life and say some of those things about me.

As I look back over the years, it makes me sad that the short-legged boy grew up. As I got older, other things became more important and a simple race in a leaf-covered yard with my Nanny lost its magic. Too bad. I wish I were six again, and we were in your back yard, ankle-deep in red, brown and yellow leaves and you were going, "Ready? Set. GO!"

Maybe this time I could let you win.

The Man on the Track

. . . For your Father knows what you need before you ask him. Pray then in this way . . .

—Matthew 6:8b-9a

More often than I care to admit I'll hit my knees in the morning and, instead of praying, "Thy will, not mine, be done," I say, "Okay God, here's what I want today. Hope you let me get by with it."

I'm not always so self-centered. It's a good thing; otherwise, this story would never have taken place. My self-centeredness plays a big part in the early part of this story.

I was alone, sitting cross-legged on the most remote corner of our activities compound, trying to get as far away from people as I could. I was learning to meditate, focusing on some Hebrew phrases. All alone on the back side of the prison, I felt God was there with me.

Minutes later, a solitary walker appeared out of the corner of my eye, approaching *my* little corner of the world. I felt my body stiffen. It was an older man, around fifty, walking the half-mile, gravel track that circles our ballfield. On his previous lap, I'd noticed him looking over at me as if he wanted to stop and say something. This time there was no doubt in my mind that he planned to stop. As he drew closer, I could feel him looking at me, and I lost what little God-concentration I had and began focusing on him and his unwelcome, uninvited intrusion. By the time I could hear his footsteps, my resentment increased, and I knew he was going to stop and talk. Couldn't he see I wanted to be alone? I was trying to be close to God and didn't have time to spend in chatter. But he didn't have anything better to do than walk around in circles and stare at me. I snuck a peek at him and knew by his haircut and the look on his face that he'd just arrived. Maybe he didn't know the rules yet, number one being, "mind your own business." I made up my mind that when he stopped I was going to give him a lesson in prison etiquette.

Not only was he about to break one of prison's unwritten rules, he was about to impose on me, and I was a self-proclaimed spiritual giant. I'd written a month of meditations for a bible-based daily meditation booklet and won a third place AMY Award in the annual writing contest for Christian writers published in the secular media. I'd met with a little success and, after a lifetime of screwing up, the results were hard to handle graciously. There were times I forgot it was all God's doing and thought I'd done something. My cell-partner, Mike, would often tell people, "We're triple-celled. It's me, Bo, and Bo's ego." He wasn't far off.

The intruder was almost upon me. I stared hard at the ground, focusing on a leaf. Were I staring at the leaf in wonderment, that would be one thing, but I was staring at the leaf in a show of concentration, hoping that when he walked up on me he would finally get it through his dense head that I wanted to be alone.

I was ready. As soon as he opened his mouth, I was going to jerk my head up, and let him have it. I tensed.

"Hey buddy? Are you okay?" he asked.

What? What was this? I expected intrusion, but nothing about his voice was intrusive.

"Yeah. Yeah, man. I'm okay. Thanks." I looked up into his eyes. All of a sudden, I felt pretty bad.

"Well, I thought maybe you wanted to talk or something. I didn't know if you were sad or what. Sorry." He started to leave.

"Hey, wait. It's okay, man. I'm just sitting here, praying and meditating. I appreciate your kindness."

"Sure. Well, look, maybe I'll see you around later? My name's Marvin." He turned, smiled and walked away.

"Hey, my name's Bo. Take care Marvin." As I watched him walking away—a peace settled down over me, and I realized I'd just had a holy encounter.

"I hear you God," I said out loud, thinking that if left on my own, I'd have told him to bug off and leave me alone, missing that whole point. I'd been so caught up in what I thought was a holy, spiritual exercise, and this man simplified the whole thing. He'd shown me a Godly person. It's good to find secluded spots to pray, but life is not about hiding in secret places and not sharing God's love with others. I suddenly realized that if Jesus had been out walking that day, he would have stopped to ask me if I was okay. With that realization

came an even more enlightening message: "He was, and he did."

Even if that had been the last time I saw Marvin, this would still be a good story, and he would have had an impact on my life; however, it wasn't the last time I saw him, nor the last time he taught me more about God and prayer.

Marvin was in the prison visiting room standing at the large, safety-glass window that looks out past the double, electronic doors that separate the visiting room from the outside world. I've stood there many a time, battling pain, fear and self-pity, as I watched people I love walk away.

Marvin was crying, watching his wife Pat go.

I got up and went to him. He'd already turned away and was walking back to the room where prisoners are "shaken down" after each visit. He was drying his eyes when he saw me. I never will forget his look.

"It's hard." He was trying hard to smile. That was the way Marvin was—in the middle of tremendous pain, he was trying to be cheerful for me, his brand-new friend.

"It'll be okay, Marvin." I nodded my head in agreement and put a sympathetic hand on his shoulder.

"Thanks." He smiled again, sniffed and walked into the shakedown room.

Prison is difficult for most people. There are exceptional cases, like the extremely hard-hearted person. But for the most part, prison is painful for everyone. Some of us have lived a pretty rough life, and the callousness and unnaturalness are not as much a shock as they were to Marvin. He had been a businessman, college educated, played basketball in college. (I can still hear him telling me how he scored forty points in a game against some powerhouse, all the while watching Pat as she looked up at him with nothing but pure love.) He was in prison because he stole money. Stealing is wrong.

Our paths crossed a lot. I'd see Marvin every morning as I walked by the chapel on my way to my job. It got to be where I could count on seeing him every morning, kneeling at a pew, head down, mouth moving. It was a powerful sight.

I run. I began about a year after I sobered up. Before long, I began to realize the physical benefits of a regular cardiovascular and aerobic exercise. Not long after I began to see some of the mental and spiritual benefits of running. One of the guys who taught me a lot about running used to say, "You can't run and worry at the same time."

I used to see Marvin as I ran. Huffing and puffing, I'd see him ahead of me, walking the track, just like on that first day. I wonder how many other people he has encountered on the track.

One day as I jogged by him I heard him say something. I really didn't feel like he had been talking *to* me, but I felt like he was talking about me. The next time I came up on his back he did it again. So the next time around I listened closer. I just knew, whatever it was he was saying, that it had something to do with me. I felt a little silly but I couldn't shake the feeling.

As I came up on his backside I could tell that he was talking, and since there was no one around, I knew he was praying. As soon as I passed by his side, he saw me. I heard his voice rise an octave or two, but I still couldn't hear what he was saying.

About twenty feet after I passed him, I *felt* it. There was suddenly no doubt in my mind that Marvin's words were connected to me. In my heart, I was certain he'd been praying for me. Chills ran all over my body.

The next time I saw him, I decided to ask him. I was tired of wondering.

"Marvin?" I began. "The other day, when I was running, well, when I passed you, I felt like you were praying for me. Were you?"

He smiled. "I pray for you every time you pass me on that track, Bo."

Although I didn't (still don't) understand everything, I knew I was witnessing something holy. It wasn't just the joyous moments I witnessed. Time and time again, I watched Marvin stand at that window as Pat left. Somehow, seeing the pain in his love for her helped me to embrace my own painful moments, knowing for the first time in my life that pain wasn't something I had to be afraid of.

One night, I looked up and there he was, sitting all alone over against the wall. I didn't see Pat and wondered what he was doing in the visiting room by himself. I went over and asked him.

"I'm leaving."

"What?"

"Yeah, they just came and told me. I'm going to a minimum-security prison."

"All right! That's great."

"Yeah, but I'm gonna miss you."

"I know, man. I know."

I bought Marvin a candy bar, hugged him and told him to take care of himself. Then I returned to the table and went on with my visit.

"You know," I told my visitor, "I think this is the first time I can remember seeing someone leave where I haven't felt jealous. I'm truly happy for Marvin."

Then I heard chains rattling, and I looked up.

Marvin, handcuffed and shackled, was shuffling his

way out the door. The same door he'd stood at so many times watching Pat walk out. He looked my way and smiled.

Tears welled in me. I cried. I cried for all the times he'd cried, cried because I was sad I wasn't going to minimum security. I cried because I was afraid I may never walk out those doors. I cried because sometimes life hurts.

I cried because I was going to miss my friend. I hope he still prays for me.

The Juror

Father, forgive them, for they know not what they do.
—Luke 23:34

His muddy white pickup rolled to a stop in the parking lot of the Circle N Quick Stop. He lifted one hip a bit and reached for his bandanna. A voice on the radio recited a Bible verse, something about "loving those who persecute you." He didn't feel like being preached to, so he turned off his radio and the Sunday morning radio preacher went silent. Taking the key from the ignition wasn't necessary, people didn't steal cars in Coalgate unless they were drunk or on drugs. He ran the dirty old bandanna across his dust-and-sweat-streaked forehead and sighed. If you'd been watching him, you might've sworn you saw the wrinkles disappear for a moment. But they came back. They always did.

Swinging one long leg out of the truck, he almost had his six-foot-one frame off the seat and out of the truck. But he stopped, leaving one foot on the ground, one on the floorboard. He reached up on the dash and picked up the picture. Sure was a good-looking man. He bit his lip. It was hard. It'd been hard for the last eleven years. Now it seemed downright unfair. He put the picture back and got out of the truck. It was one of those perfect, mid-May Oklahoma days. The sun was posted up in an endless clear blue sky, but his spirit was too cloudy to notice.

As he walked into the store, he failed to notice who was working the cash register. He made an immediate left turn, away from the check-out counter toward the back of the store where the beer was. He wasn't going to get beer. He hadn't had a drink in over seven years. He was getting a half-gallon of milk to take home. As he walked by the beer coolers, he overheard two young men discussing how much and what kind of beer they would buy. He knew their dads and felt a passing urge to stop and tell the boys there was a better way, and it wasn't in the bottom of a beer can, but he also knew that sometimes it took what it took, and no amount of intervention could change the course of events. He thought about the man in the picture on his dashboard and wondered if, eleven years ago, anyone had thought about stopping him and offering him a better way.

He reached in the cooler with his tan, weathered hand, scratched from the limbs he'd been hauling all day, and got his milk. When he turned around, his stomach tightened. There, behind the counter, was another one. They were everywhere. Well, maybe not everywhere, but he couldn't spend half day in town without seeing one. That shouldn't have been surprising; Coalgate was a small town, and there was a good chance that, out of a group of twelve jurors, you'd run into one of them each day.

By the time he reached the counter, his blood was

boiling. He stood in line, glaring at her, watching her stick a long, red-tipped cigarette in her mouth and suck on it until her cheeks hollowed out. It looked like salvation itself was somewhere in that cigarette. He struggled to stop shaking.

He remembered another time, in another check-out line at another small town quick stop. He'd been dressed much like he was today—dirty brown boots, dusty jeans, sweaty work shirt and stained straw hat. It was what he wore when he fed cattle, and he usually didn't have time to get his feeding done, shower and change and still have time to make that three-hour round trip.

That day, he'd been on the first leg of the trip and had stopped for a small sack of stuffed jalapeno peppers, cheese sticks and chicken strips. That was the meal the two of them had been sharing for some time. That same weathered hand held onto a small, grease-stained sack as he waited for the cashier to finish with two locals. There was a small black and white TV behind the counter. The news was on.

"Hey, could you turn that up?" the man in front of him said to the cashier. Everyone stopped to listen to the anchorman tell how the legislature had passed another bill authorizing the spending of more money to build prisons. It was a last-ditch effort to stop the "revolving door" and stem the crime problem.

"Hell, it's about time they did something about those prisons. They need to lock those no-goods up and throw away the key. That's what they need to do," said the man in front of him. His sentiment was echoed by the handful of locals. Everyone had something to say except the dust-covered man with the sweat-stained shirt holding his little sack.

Five years later, here he was again; another line in another quick stop, this time in his own hometown. He remembered how he'd kept his eyes on his boot tops five years ago as he'd paid. He hadn't wanted to look up and meet the gaze of the cashier or the people in line, but he knew if he did, he'd say something that he would regret.

Now, once again, he found himself in the same situation. The closer he got to the front of the line, the more his heart pounded. He felt hate. He felt rage. He felt repulsed, sick.

He handed the woman his money and stared at her.

"Jim." She nodded her head in greeting.

Nothing. He continued to stare.

She handed him his change and with a snort of disgust, he turned his glare from her and walked out the door. When he was safely outside, he took a breath. By the time he got to his truck, he had stopped shaking. That's when it hit him. He didn't want to feel like that any more. He was tired of hating people, holding resentments. The poison of all those stored hurts was beginning to tell. He sat down in his pickup and put his head in his big hands.

It wasn't a conscious decision. He reached up, grabbed the picture and was halfway across the parking lot before he wondered if it was the right thing to do.

"Georgina, I apologize. I'm sorry for my attitude the last eleven years. You just don't know how much it hurts. But I'm wrong, and I owe you and all the others an apology—a real one."

"Oh, Jim, I'm sorry too. I understand how . . ." she started to say.

"No, you don't. Please don't even say that. You don't understand." He laid the picture on the counter.

"Oh." It was a small sound. She knew it was a picture, and she knew who was in it.

"That's him. I thought maybe if you saw him, you could at least see why I'm angry, and why I react the way I do. Look at him."

She had a hard time forcing her gaze down. The young man in the black and white picture had barely been old enough to drink the last time she saw him. Now he was thirty-three years old. Looking at him unsettled her; there was something about him. The young man looked normal enough, even good-looking, but that wasn't it. The last thing he looked like was a prisoner, much less a murderer. It bothered her, looking into those smiling, peaceful, almost black eyes gazing out from the 5 x 7 picture. What disturbed her was not physical. Suddenly, she knew.

"Jim, we were told that he'd be out in seven years. I'd never have voted *guilty* if I'd known."

"Well," he reached across the counter and grabbed the picture. "I just wanted you to see him. I thought maybe it would help you to understand. He doesn't belong in there. Maybe he did once, but not anymore."

"I'm so sorry," she said, returning her eyes to the counter.

"Well, me too." He turned to leave.

"I guess you'll always hate us, won't you?" She asked.

"No, I won't. I'm working on it." He walked out into the parking lot. His bottom lip trembled. Taking his straw hat off with his other hand, he raised his face into the sun. The light felt good. The sky was bigger and bluer than he'd ever seen it.

He looked back down at the picture of his son.

The Graduate

Perhaps the reason he was separated from you for a little while was that you might have him back for good.
—Philemon 2:15

I watched tears run down Judy's face as she put her arm around her son, Greg. That's one of the reasons I was crying. Another is that I believe in miracles, and I was seeing one.

Greg was graduating from the Lifeline Substance Abuse Treatment Program, a prison treatment center funded in part by the Norman Alcohol Information Center, a non-profit agency funded in part by the Episcopal Church. I'd graduated from the same program six years earlier and lived in the treatment housing unit helping out as a peer counselor.

Greg and my cell partner, Skip, and another close friend, David, were graduating. I shaved, put my hair up in a ponytail and went. As I was putting on my blue denim prison-issue shirt, I wondered what the keynote speaker, Senator Cal Hobson, would say. A lot had changed since the last time I'd heard him.

That time, Hobson made many inferences,

mentioned completion of treatment and getting out of prison in the same sentences. The political climate had changed. People weren't getting out of prison early in Oklahoma. It made no difference if you went up for parole with an active drug habit or a college degree— no one was getting out early. It would be interesting to see what the Senator said. Even though he was an out-spoken advocate of education and treatment in prison, surely he couldn't deny reality. The Governor, the government, the media, the public, the majority of Oklahoma citizens had vengeance on their minds when considering prisons and the people who live here.

I walked into the prison visiting room and found Greg and his family. For a moment I thought they'd brought Greg's entire hometown. Everyone was there: grandma, grandpa, aunts, uncles, nieces, nephews, sister, dad and mom. They were proud of Greg, and they had a right to be. He'd been a first-person participant in a miracle. After ten years of heavy drug and alcohol addiction, he was clean and sober.

Like most of us, he wasn't as much a criminal as a person who gave drugs and alcohol control of his life.

I remember the first time my mom saw Greg. She looked shocked. "My goodness, he's just a child." She had a point. Greg looked like a college freshman. If you take away the shirts with *Oklahoma Corrections* stenciled across the back, most of us aren't identifiable as convicts.

Senator Hobson began his speech. I took my first glance down front where Greg and his mom sat. I thought of the first time I'd met him. He and I played softball, our first common interest. Back then, that was just about it. He was still into getting high, and I was into getting clean. I liked him. His boyish good looks, his magnanimous glow and ever-present smile, made it hard not to like him. We became friends.

A couple years later, my friend cleaned up and, now, here I was at his commencement. Hobson was telling us how our actions affect so much more than just us. He was speaking of the negative effects of drug and alcohol abuse on others; how we often think we're the only one. ("But Mom," I can still hear myself say, "I'm not hurting anyone. Why don't you just leave me alone?") As I took another glance at Greg and his mom, especially the look on her face when she'd turn her gaze toward him, I was touched by the depth of her joy. The Jewish Talmud says that God couldn't be everywhere, so he made mothers.

It was suddenly crystal-clear that God must be a lot like a mom. Jesus' words about the lost sheep and the prodigal son came alive as I watched Judy look at Greg with love so pure. It was a holy moment. A healing was taking place.

I turned my attention back to the Senator. He told us that every morning he sat down at the local coffee shop and listened to the townsfolk complain about people in prison receiving education, medical treatment, substance abuse treatment, even food. The majority of society wants us punished, not pampered.

Taking another glance at Greg and his mom, I wondered what those same hard-liners would say if they could see what I saw.

Hobson wound up his speech. The graduates received certificates and a small, bronze medal that said,

"One day at a time." One by one, they got up and shook hands with the Warden, the Senator, the Director of Lifeline. Plenty of applause, mixed with whistles, hoots and hollers, followed each one of them across the floor. They beat the odds, and everyone knew it.

When they called Greg's name, I watched his mom. She didn't bother to wipe the tears from her face. By the time Greg sat down, I was crying too. I couldn't help it.

Hobson must've noticed Greg's mom because I saw him walk over to Judy. "He's going to be okay," I read his lips as he put a hand on her shoulder.

"I know." I saw her answer, nodding her head.

When she reached out to her son and pulled him into her arms, I knew, too.

*   *   *

Epilogue. Within two months, Greg fell prey to the numbers game in our overcrowded prison and was shipped to a private prison in Texas, miles away from his mom and his dad. The night they told him he was being shipped, he came to our cell to tell Skip and me. Fear was all over his young face. He was afraid for his mom and dad, and he was afraid about his sobriety. He didn't say it; he didn't have to. I turned on my computer and opened this story and let him read it. When he finished, he looked up, cleared his throat, and said, "Man, I'm going to be all right."

Is Anybody Out There?

I call aloud upon the Lord; and he answers me from his holy hill. —Psalm 3:4

God is not a cosmic bellboy for whom we can press a button to get things done. —Harry Emerson Fosdick

Not long ago I heard a friend exclaim: "I just want God to send me a good woman." And a second man replied, "Send God a *Request to Staff.*"

Most of my prayer life has resembled leafing through a Neiman Marcus Christmas catalog. My prayer life has been a long list of "I wants." When I'm not busy presenting God with a shopping list, I often say, "Okay, God, get me out of this one, and *I promise* I won't do *that* again."

From my present vantage point, atop a single bunk bed, looking at four concrete walls, a steel door, and a window with a view of double twelve-foot razor-wire fence designed to keep me here forever, it appears God hasn't heard my last "get me out of this one" prayer.

Looking around the cell that Skip and I share, it's pretty obvious God hasn't been to Neiman Marcus either.

My question is: Why bother? It's pretty obvious prayer doesn't work as well as religious folk want to believe. If it did, I'd be home, flopped on the couch. As it is, my home is the state prison, and the only couch I'm likely to see today is this bunk bed.

Prayers. Do they work? All the time? Sometimes? Only certain prayer? What's the deal?

His name is Moses, and his picture is on my wall. Moses used to come here as a volunteer, back in the late eighties and early nineties and taught me the meaning of the word "holy." He showed me I could be a sensitive, spiritual person, have a real relationship with my creator, and not be a dogmatic zealot, condemning everyone who failed to believe what I believed. He taught me this and much more. Moses showed me how to walk in love. And he taught me about prayer.

Every time Moses left, we would stop at the front gate, put our arms around each other, bow our heads together in a tight little circle and pray. We didn't pray for material things; we prayed for spiritual things—love, peace, joy and faith.

During one of Moses' visits his wife was in critical condition following surgery. He told us he'd been sitting at the hospital, worrying and praying, afraid to leave, when he felt a need to come to prison. So, he drove out to tell us what was going on and ask for our prayers.

The next week after he gave us the news that his wife had pulled through and was going to be fine, he told us that the week before, on the way home from prison, he had experienced an overwhelming assurance that she was okay. He realized that he had been instructed to leave the hospital and go to our prison. As I sat and listened, I shivered. It wasn't cold.

Moses told us that as a result of the complications she suffered, the doctors said she would never be able to have children. Two years later, Moses again asked for our prayers, this time requesting God's help in having a baby. I thought he was pushing it, but Moses seemed to believe. That helped me to believe.

Again, we prayed. I even asked Moses, joking, what he wanted: a boy or girl?

That picture of Moses on my wall shows him holding Zara, his two-year old daughter.

Not too long ago a man approached me as I was about to begin a work out. He works out too, so this was not out of the ordinary. We often talked, trading bits of information and advice on the less than perfect science of getting in shape. This time something was different.

"Hey, man." I said. "What's up?"

"I've been looking for you."

"What's going on?"

His lip started trembling as he tried to open his mouth and tell me. Nothing came out.

"What's going on brother? What is it?"

"It's my Mom," he finally managed to whisper. "She's got a tumor."

He sobbed, and I couldn't do anything but reach out and put my hand on his shoulder.

"I'm sorry," was my weak reply. What could I say?

"I came to ask you to pray for her." He looked straight into my eyes.

Why me? I thought, but the look in his eyes commanded respect, and I said, "Sure. What's her name?"

He told me, dried his eyes and walked off leaving me standing there wondering: why me? I really like him and consider him one of my favorite people, but he and I are not close friends. We talk when we see each other, but we don't hang out together. We've talked of spiritual matters before, but not often. Why me? It kept going through my thoughts.

That night as I prayed, I asked God to heal his mother and to comfort him and the family. As soon as the words escaped my lips, the neatest thing happened. Let me explain that I'm a bit uncomfortable telling you that God spoke to me, but the minute those words left my mouth I felt, more than I heard, "It's okay."

I knew she was going to be okay. Of course, the doubt set in when I realized that in believing that I'd heard this answer, I was saying God had spoken to me. Would I tell anyone? I couldn't deny the certainty of what I'd experienced, but at the same time, I don't usually tell people God talks to me. Still, I had to tell the guy.

I saw him the next day.

"Guess what? Last night when I prayed, I, well, uh, man, I feel kinda weird saying this, but I swear it's the truth . . . anyway . . . last night when I prayed, I got this feeling, but it was more than a feeling, it was, like, well, like God said, 'It's okay.'" And then I went on, "I promise, I wouldn't go around saying this, except, well, that's exactly what happened. I gotta tell ya."

"I believe you." That's all he said.

At this same time, I was waiting for a ruling from

the judge who sentenced me. The faith I felt concerning my friend's situation bled over into my own life and, before I knew it, I was feeling pretty certain that not only had God heard my prayers concerning my release but had the same plans for my future as I did! I knew that God had answered my prayer for my friend. Why not my prayer too?

A week later, as we were starting a softball game. I was on the mound tossing a few warm-up balls when my friend walked toward me.

"It's benign."

"All right, man." We hugged each other.

"Well, I better let you go. You guys are about to start. I just wanted you to know. Thanks."

"Oh no, man, don't thank me. I didn't do anything." I said.

As he walked off, I had a hard time focusing on the plate. I stood still a moment and lowered my head. I was confused. My tears were more for me than they were for him. The night before, I'd found out that the judge had turned me down. Now, I was wondering why God didn't answer *my* prayer.

"Thanks God," I whispered, genuinely grateful for my friend and his mom. And yet more than a little sad that, apparently, God hadn't answered my own prayers. Before the notion could materialize, it happened again. Almost as if God knew what my next thought was going to be, I felt, more than I heard, God say, "Be patient."

I'm trying.

Just A Game

No discipline seems pleasant at the time, but painful. Later on, however, it produces a harvest of righteousness and peace for those who have been trained by it.
                                          —Hebrews 12:11

Football. It does something to me. Each fall brings with it renewed energy and a hopeful reminder. Despite the fact that it's just a game, it happens to be where I learned about life.

As with any lesson, there must be a teacher and mine was a short, stocky man with short, dark, wavy hair, smiling eyes, gray polyester coaches' shorts and a huge heart. The football field in my hometown is named after him, and although I haven't seen Mayer Field in a long time, hardly a day goes by that I don't think about the man: Coach Donald Mike Mayer.

Halfway through my freshman year in high school, our 9th grade team was undefeated. Meanwhile, across the field where the high school team practiced, it was a different story. They were struggling through a winless season, but watching them practice you couldn't tell they hadn't won a game. Each week, it seemed, they practiced harder and with more enthusiasm than they had the week before. It baffled me and my teammates, who thought winning was the only goal. But that was before I played for Coach Mayer.

Earlier that year, a couple of my more gifted teammates had been asked to play on the undermanned high school team and even though they went out and lost every Friday night, something about them changed. It was more than just the confidence that comes with being better than your classmates; they'd had that ever since we were in grade school. This was a different kind of confidence. I just assumed that, being an average athlete, I would find out what it was like to play for Coach Mayer the following year. But when our season was over, I was asked to play on the high school team.

That was the biggest honor bestowed on me in my brief athletic career, and I was more than happy to spend my weekday afternoons being pummeled and trod upon by the bigger and stronger upperclassmen. It was a thrill to be a part of the longer, harder practices, and every day I survived I began to carry myself a little differently.

I prefer to think that it must've showed in my performance and it wasn't simply because they were running out of warm bodies that Coach Mayer told me I would be starting at safety with three games left in the season.

"Get that grin off your face. This is serious," he told me. I tried but it wouldn't go away.

Over the course of the next three weeks, I was run over, run by and smashed flat by bigger, faster and stronger players and even though I didn't know Coach Mayer as well as I would come to know him over the next two years, I did know that all he expected of me was to get back up. I did. Over and over.

I couldn't stop grinning. I was so thrilled to be a part of the team that even in the middle of a game I'd be grinning from ear to ear. I'd come to the sideline to get a play or receive instructions, pulling grass out of my face mask from where I'd been steamrolled, and I'd be grinning.

"Get that grin off your face," he'd say again. But by now, he was getting used to me because he was starting to smile too. I didn't know it at the time but that smile was slated to play a large part in the rest of my life.

The next football season wasn't much different. We managed to win two games. But we practiced harder each week. I continued to learn about heart, discipline and getting back up when you're knocked down. Coach Mayer didn't just preach these qualities, he exemplified them. When we were dogging it, he'd outrun us in windsprints. When someone couldn't understand a certain blocking technique, he'd get down in a four-point stance and fire off the line into a fully-padded, usually surprised, student.

When he said something, he meant it. He was one of only two coaches I've known who treated star players exactly the same way he treated the benchwarmers. His word was gold. I remember watching in amazement as he paddled our best wide receiver for cussing after he'd dislocated his finger and yelled a few choice words. There was no cussing on Coach Mayer's teams, even if you dislocated a finger. A rule was a rule, he said, as he administered the swats with what can only be described as love.

There was no pretense. What you saw was what you got. He coached football, but he also taught life, and although I doubt there was a single one of us who doubted his integrity or lacked respect for him, none of us had any idea how much more we had to learn.

One day, he walked into the dressing room and told us he had something to say. You could tell by the look on his face this was something serious.

"Guys, I'm sick. It seems I've got a disease called amyotrophic lateral sclerosis. It's also known as Lou Gehrig's disease. Right now, I'm pretty much okay, just some numbness. But, they tell me that it's going to get worse. I don't know how long it'll take, or how long I'll be able to do this. If you guys and the coaching staff want me to, I'll continue as long as I can." It was clear to see that he was scared to death and it scared us, seeing the man we knew as the epitome of courage so obviously frightened. He stayed.

ALS is a degenerative disease of the muscles. At first it's felt as numbness and gradually works its way through the body, taking with it control of the muscles. Within weeks, Coach Mayer was slurring his speech and having noticeable trouble with his motor capabilities.

It became difficult to hear what he was saying and even more painful to see the frustration and anger on his face, as he fought against this invisible entity that was slowly robbing him of his life.

If we had thought he'd taught us about courage and determination before, now we were learning on a whole new level. Getting back up when you've been knocked down took a whole new meaning one day when, during a scrimmage he was knocked down by a sweeping running back who didn't see him. If he had stayed on the sideline, he'd have been okay, but that wasn't his way. He was right out there like he'd always been, smack dab in the middle of action.

It was like slow motion, watching him fall to the ground. He couldn't get his arms out to break his fall and landed flat on his back with a loud groan. His head whipped backward, bouncing off the ground and I though it'd knocked him out until he made a noise. We rushed to help him up but he waved us off with an angry grunt as he struggled to get up by himself. The look on his face is still with me. For a long time I thought he was mad at us for knocking him down, but then I realized he was mad at something much more. He was dying on his feet.

By the time the season came to an end, he was forced to coach from a golf cart. It was chaos on the sidelines as the assistant coaches struggled to understand him and marveled at his doggedness.

Finally, the last game arrived, and although we weren't good enough to do it, since we knew we were playing our last game under Coach Mayer, we told him we were going to win it for him. He knew we weren't physically capable of winning, but he also wanted to go out a winner, and he managed to twist his face into a faint smile when we told him what we were going to do.

We put up a brave fight, staying in the game, but eventually we gave way to a better team and lost the last game he coached. That in itself was bad, but nothing compared to what happened after the game. Each one of us came up to him and told him we were sorry, and while he nodded and managed to mumble "It's okay," it was clear to see in his eyes that it wasn't okay. Then he went in his office with the assistant coaches and shut the door.

While we were showering and dressing, it happened. The most heartbreaking sound I've ever heard came from behind that closed door. At first, it sounded like a wounded animal. Coach Mayer was crying.

I couldn't stand it. I hurried up and dressed so I could leave. Before I could get out, one of the assistant coaches came out and his wet, red eyes hinted what was taking place behind that door.

During the remainder of the school year, I'd see Coach occasionally. He'd come up to the school for something, or I'd see him at a basketball game. But, he had retired. That summer the school board hired a new football coach.

That was also the summer I began drinking and using drugs. Occasionally some of us guys would get together and go out to Coach Mayer's house to visit him. We never stayed long. It was uncomfortable to see him sitting in bed with a bib around his neck instead of a whistle. And, even though he could barely talk with his mouth, his eyes still spoke to me. I remember thinking that, somehow, he knew I'd been smoking weed and drinking and those piercing eyes made me ashamed. Today, I wonder if he was mad at me for having good health and taking it for granted.

The next year we both continued into a slow but steady downward spiral, only thing was mine was optional. I still visited occasionally and I still left feeling guilty.

The first game of my senior year was special for me and for Coach Mayer. He still came to all the home games. His wife would drive him to a designated place on the sideline, and he would watch the game from the front seat of his four-wheel drive pickup. He'd been to all the games our junior year, the year after he retired, but his health had deteriorated to the point that no one knew how much longer he'd be able to continue. But he was there that first game.

We were playing the defending state champs, a perennial powerhouse. That same group of freshmen who had gotten their start under Coach Mayer were now seniors and although they'd struggled through a couple of two-win seasons since, they remembered that they had been undefeated as a class three years ago.

The game was back and forth and every time we'd take the lead I'd look over at the sidelines where that four-wheel-drive truck sat. In the huddle, we reminded each other who was over there watching us. Finally, tied at the end of regulation, we went into overtime. They got the ball first and we held them.

On our first play we scored, and as soon as we untangled ourselves from the pile in the end zone, a group of us trotted over to where he was parked.

"Hey, Coach. We did it."

"I know," he mouthed and nodded his head. Tears were running down his face.

And he smiled.

I Don't Want to Be His Brother

If anyone says, "I love God," yet hates his brother, he is a liar.
                                                    —1 John 4:20

Two or three times a summer we have a picnic; wicker basket, blanket—the works. On one particular picnic, I even had a woman companion. It was a beautiful summer day. She and I were lying back, half-reclined, her head on my chest, staring up into my face. Few days in prison were like this one.

Suddenly a guard appeared. "You can't be like that," he said.

"Whaddya mean? We're not doing anything," I shot back.

"Sit up straight."

"C'mon man," I pleaded. "I've been here almost ten years and we've always been able to lie around as long as we're not being inappropriate." His look told me it wasn't about right or wrong; it was about power.

"You heard me," he said with a sneer and walked off.

After he left, we again settled into a comfortable pose, somewhat modified from our first position. Another guard walked up.

"You can't sit like that, either."

"C'mon, y'all ain't right," I said, feeling my face begin to get hot.

"You heard me."

We sat up and watched her walk off. She marched directly to the first guard, and they high-fived each other and laughed.

We were furious. Fortunately, the warden happened to be there, we found him and told him what had happened.

"Warden, we are grown people. We know what's appropriate behavior. These guys are way outta line," I said.

He said he would take care of the situation and told us not to worry. We returned to our blanket and our own private world.

"I've already told you two to sit up."

"Look, we talked to the warden, and he said we could lie back, so why don't you go ask him," I replied. It was my turn to smirk.

He looked at me a moment, trying to decide whether I was bluffing, decided I wasn't, and stomped off. The woman and I enjoyed a very special afternoon.

Later that evening, the guard came back. "Sit up," he ordered.

"Look man, the warden . . ." I began.

"The warden is gone and I said SIT UP," he ordered.

"You're wrong," I said.

"What'd you say?"

"I said you're wrong."

He let out a stream of profanity and told us to get up, that our visit was terminated. He proceeded to get on his walkie-talkie and call for backup.

"Why?" She asked him. "We didn't do anything."

"He's not gonna cuss me like that," he answered.

"He didn't cuss you. I didn't cuss you," she said.

"Get your stuff gathered up."

"Look, pal, you're the one who started cussing. Just because you're wrong, and we called you on it, you can't treat us like this."

"I can do what I want. Gather your stuff up."

I was angry. The guard was abusing us and there was nothing I could do about it. I was dying inside. We get to spend two days a week with visitors. We live for those two days. I began to beg.

"Look, I'm sorry. Please don't terminate our visit."

He mumbled something about not letting it happen again and he walked off. I was relieved, though angry and humiliated.

That next Monday I was called into my Unit Manager's office and told that there had been a serious incident report filed on me.

"What happened?" the Unit Manager asked.

I told him and then he showed me the report. I was incensed. "Sam, those are bold-faced lies," I sputtered. He must have believed me because nothing was ever said about it. It should've been over.

It wasn't. For the next month, every time I saw that guard, I wanted to tell him what I thought of him. The longer I stared at him, the more my blood pressure rose. I became almost physically ill every time I saw him or thought about him. I deeply resented the man.

Days later, getting ready for a visit, I saw him. Resentment poured from me. Within minutes, I was shaking. The intensity of my response alarmed me. I had to do something, but what?

Five years earlier, at the beginning of my sobriety, I was told that if I wanted to get rid of a resentment, I should pray for the person I resented. I didn't have to feel it. All I had to do was pray, to say the words, ask God to give that person every good thing that I could want for myself. I knew it worked. I'd done it for people I mildly resented. This time, I felt justified in my anger. Why should I ask for anything? He was the one who was clearly wrong. It was cut and dried. I had been wronged; my anger was justified.

But I'd also been told that resentments cut you off from the sunlight of the Spirit. It hit me how true this is. In the midst of my righteous indignation, I didn't feel a drop of love. My anger was making me miserable, threatening my relationships, and not bothering the guard one bit.

Still, I wasn't willing to do it. As miserable as I was, I couldn't bring myself to give in to the small, calm voice that was telling me to give it up. Thankfully, that voice didn't relent.

I dropped to my knees and said, "God, please give that man everything good that I desire. Please God, please." I meant it. It was an earnest prayer not because I liked the guy, but I was desperate. I had to find peace.

As the words left my mouth, I felt relief flood over

me and I knew this way worked. On my knees I wasn't alone. Not only could I pray for small resentments, I could pray for a situation that filled me with hatred and rage.

Rage and hatred are powerful emotions. Once they get their claws into you, it is very hard to get free. Rage and hatred wait to come back. Before long, I thought about the guard and discovered I still felt very angry. But now there was a solution. I knew prayer would work, even if only a moment at a time. So, day by day, and sometimes minute by minute, I continued to pray.

At first, all it did was get me through to the next moment. I'd see him, get mad, pray, feel better and then he'd be gone. After a short while, the strangest thing happened, almost without my noticing it. Before I knew it, I was saying "Hi" to him and asking him how he was doing. I meant it.

I still fight against the notion that this man is my brother. But, deep down in the place where truth lives inside me, there is a whisper, and if I listen closely, a gentle voice is telling me he is. Sometimes, I'm able to believe it.

Deb's Mail-order Groom

Whoever finds a wife finds a good thing and obtains favor from the LORD. —Proverbs 18:22

It was hot the day I received her letter in July, in Oklahoma, in prison. It wasn't the only letter handed me through the window of the mail room that day, but out of the handful it was the one I remember. I carried it with me for a hundred yards, holding it in my hands, turning it over, analyzing it, as if I could judge its contents by its weight or the handwriting on the front. It was heavy; the handwriting was neat. Deborah F. Rogers, whoever she was, had neat handwriting and had written me more than a page. Other than that and the postmark, I knew nothing about this letter or the person who sent it.

Prison mail call is an experience all to itself. After thirteen years, I'm still as excited as a twelve-year-old on Christmas morning whenever I see my name on the mail list. Who wrote? Is it good news? Is it someone I haven't heard from in a while? Could it be something to do with getting out of prison? Could it be money? The possibilities are endless.

The one thing I did know was that Deborah Rogers was a woman and that captured my interest. Rubbing elbows with a thousand men every day gets old very fast. I was cautious in my optimism.

A few years earlier I'd met a woman, and she'd quickly swept me off my feet, and we were married in prison. For the first few months of the relationship, I was happy. Then things changed. The person I thought I knew turned out to be a stranger. Many lies and more than one lover later, she said she had made a mistake to marry me. It was over.

I was crushed and swore never to fall in love again. Women were off-limits for me. I wouldn't even smile at one of *them* as long as I remained in prison. Maybe never. The break-up depressed me. When I finally came through that valley with my sanity, spirituality and serenity intact, I knew it had to do with God's grace.

As I held the letter in my hand, I felt ready for what-ever it contained. Most likely, it wasn't anything. Over the years my mail had not been the stereo-typical prisoner's fare. Ever since I'd written a series of medi-tations for Forward Movement, I'd been deluged with mail from all over the United States. More often than not, they were from people who described themselves as being old enough to be my grandparent or parent. Whole families wanted to let me know they appreci-ated my efforts. Those letters continue to be among the most rewarding facets of my existence.

But I knew the one in my hand was different. Maybe it was hope, maybe premonition, maybe my biological clock was overriding the rest of my system. My palms were moist and my breath did a little stutterstep when I pulled the folded letter out of the number 10 envelope.

"Dear Bo Cox," it began. Ms. Rogers was the secretary of an Episcopal Church in Kentucky. She'd been flipping through the spring '97 Forward Movement catalog, saw my picture and felt drawn to me. Flattering as that was, red flags were waving in the hot July wind. My failed marriage had been love at first sight. I had no intention of again handing my heart to someone.

Though her letter was safe and antiseptic, I could read between the lines. The message I was getting flirted with kindling a fire I thought extinguished.

I must have read her letter ten times that evening. Deborah had asked me questions which went beyond usual first letter protocol. She had cut to the quick and wanted to know what I thought about our country's criminal justice system, including not-so-simple issues like the death penalty. She'd made a trip to jail during a junior high school field trip, and when the prisoners had jumped up to the bars and begun taunting her and her class with crude, sexual epithets she'd formed her own opinions about prisons and how those people needed to be treated. But I didn't look like a prisoner, she wrote. She'd read some of my writings. I didn't sound like a prisoner.

She wanted to know: what *was* the real story concerning crime and punishment, prisons and the people who live there? How did I keep my faith in God? Had I been raped or assaulted? What was it like to be so hopelessly addicted to drugs? How did I manage to keep a positive attitude while doing a life sentence? Not only did she ask me probing questions, she wrote intimate details of her own life.

Soon I'd finished my response, the perfect mixture of interest and indifference. I was definitely attracted to her, and it wasn't just because she was interested in me. Yet I didn't want to step too far out into this still undefined relationship. I wanted to play it safe.

In a matter of days, she and I exchanged more letters and we began to burn up the phone lines between Oklahoma and Kentucky. Not only did I discover she was as much a country girl as I was a country boy, I fell in love with her Kentucky accent. By the third phone call I felt I was talking to an old friend.

Beyond everything, beyond the yearning for female companionship, beyond the ego stroking that comes with having it, beyond the hopeless romantic fantasy I was beginning to dream up, there was a feeling of security. In that, I felt God's hand, and it was good to feel safe.

Not only did I feel safe, I felt I had met a kindred spirit *and* a role model. In her second letter to me, Deb told me she suffered from endometriosis. Before I picked up that letter, I had no idea how to spell endometriosis, much less understand it. By the time I put that letter down, I had a basic understanding of endo, a serious condition for women, and I understood a little more about this woman. I found out she wasn't afraid of much. I found out she wouldn't run from pain. I found out she'd walked through, and conquered, more than one difficult period in her life. And, yet, she still believed in God and in God's love. She wasn't a quitter, and she wasn't a whiner. She was a woman of strong faith.

By this time we knew we were being drawn to one another. As much as I tried to convince myself—and anyone who'd listen—that we weren't going to jump into anything, I also knew that a serious relationship was developing. It was like a stone rolling downhill.

I felt a need, an obligation, to warn this very genuine and somewhat naïve woman that she was getting into a situation way over her head. Getting involved with a guy doing a life sentence is very risky. Not only was she setting herself up for pain, frustration and disillusionment, there was my heart to consider. I well knew what it felt like to go ahead and give it away, believing in the power of love to overcome reality and razor wire fences, only to have it fall short.

Because I really liked her and partly because I really liked myself, I decided I needed to paint as realistic a picture as possible. "Deb," I began, "I'm crazy about you. But, I'm also afraid you don't know what you're getting into. There's a real possibility I may never get out and, as good as this feels right now, there's gonna come a time when you get tired of the prison thing. Not only that, you're in Kentucky and I'm in Oklahoma. Even if you lived down the road from me, this would be hard. I'm not saying 'go away,' please know that, but I do have to warn you: Loving me hurts. This is going to be hard and . . . "

"Thank you, sir," she cut me off. "I appreciate your warning, or whatever it is you call that. Now, I don't want to hear it again. You've said it, and I heard you. Do you want me out of your life?"

"No, of course not," I told her. I didn't. No way.

"Well, then consider me warned. And I don't ever

want to hear those words come out of your mouth again. Okay, Mr. Cox?"

That was when I knew. Deb later told me she knew the minute she saw my picture. She told me she called her brother-in-law, Woody (the coolest Southern Baptist minister I know) and said, "Woody, I just found my man!"

Of course, Woody was incredulous. "Deb? What in the world are you talking about? What man? *How'd* you meet him?"

She told him, and he told her she was crazy. Her mom and dad didn't, though. When I learned of their reaction I knew they had to be most special people. After all, their daughter was telling them she was interested in a man serving a life sentence in an Oklahoma prison for first-degree murder. And, to top *that* off, he was an Episcopalian!

They didn't ground her. They didn't scream at her. They didn't preach to her. They didn't warn her. They advised her to put it in God's hands. I took their reaction as another sign.

We hadn't known each other for two weeks when, out of the blue, she asked if she should come to Oklahoma to see me. That appealed to me, and I told her so. I assumed she'd fly out that coming spring, or, if I got lucky, maybe even over the holidays that were months away. No, she wasn't waiting a few months, and she wasn't flying. She wanted to drive, and she wanted to do it the following week!

She left work on a Friday afternoon and went home to pack. Her plans were to leave before dark, drive all night, and arrive in Oklahoma City, forty miles from the prison, early that next morning. I called her house about nine o'clock Friday night, more to ease my nerves than anything else.

"Hello?" she answered the phone.

"What are you doing there?" I asked. All of a sudden I was afraid. I knew it was too good to be true. She was backing out.

"I'm not packed yet," she said and, as if she could read my thoughts, added, "Don't worry. I'm coming. I'll see you in the morning."

My heart leapt. You wait all your life, sometimes in vain, to hear a voice reach inside you and find a place where it fits. Her's sounded so right.

The next morning I got up at six o'clock, drank a cup of coffee and, since I was in the middle of a two month relapse after eight years of nicotine-free existence, chained-smoked cigarettes until seven. At seven, I shaved, jumped in the shower, scrubbed myself spotless and shampooed and conditioned my hair. I put on a pair of old sweats and walked around outside, enjoying a few more cigarettes, but smoking them outside where I could keep from getting the smoke all over me. At quarter 'til eight, I began scrubbing and cleansing my teeth and washing my hands and face to finish getting rid of my smoker's smell. To complete the transformation, I crammed three or four sticks of spearmint gum into my mouth and chewed them for a minute before spitting that out and adding a fresh wad. Next, I got my visiting clothes on and headed to the area in front of the visiting room to wait on my first visit with Deb.

The visiting room at the Joseph Harp Correctional

Center is separated from the waiting area on the prisoners' side by a wall of reflective glass. You can see through it if you press your face against it. Naturally, they have rules against that, but those rules didn't keep me from pressing my nose against the window like a pet store puppy waiting for someone to buy me as I looked outside for a glimpse of her.

They called the first fifteen prisoners. My name wasn't called. Then ten more. No Cox. I asked the guard if he'd somehow missed my name. He looked. No, he hadn't. Now I was starting to worry. Finally, he told me that every visitor that had been in line out front was now in the visiting room.

"Are you sure you haven't called my name?" I asked.

"Let me check. Nope."

I went back to my unit to wait. I was worried, not that I thought something had happened. I knew she was okay. I just hated being powerless. If I weren't in prison I could call the motel where she was planning on staying. But, in prison, the only calls you can make are collect calls, and a motel in Oklahoma City would not accept a collect call from a prisoner. If I weren't in prison she could have called me and told me she was running behind or had a flat or whatever the case may be.

But I was in prison. I waited.

I went back to my cell and took off my good clothes and hopped back into my old sweats so I could chain-smoke some more. I sat there, smoking and sending prayers up to heaven on my clouds of carbon monoxide and thousands of other carcinogens. Finally a guard came and told me I had a visit.

I threw my clothes back on, scrubbed my mouth,

hands and face and began walking the couple hundred yards from my cell to the visiting yard. About halfway there, I looked around to make sure no one was watching and I took off running. I was thirty-three years old and felt every bit of thirteen.

I stepped inside the small sally port separating the prison yard from the visiting room and signed the sign-in log. Then before being allowed in the visiting room, I was given a thorough search by the visiting room officer. While I was standing with my legs spread and my arms out to my side, I noticed Deb. She was sitting alone at a table. She looked small and vulnerable. She also looked scared. I found out later that she was afraid I wasn't going to like her.

As we walked across the room toward each other, I began to smile. I guess she saw my eyes because, suddenly, she broke into a smile, too. She had told me in one of her letters that as a child, one of her pet names was Sunshine, and as she smiled, it lit up her whole face.

"Let's go outside," I said. We walked out to the outside visiting area. As soon as I put my arm around her, everything felt right. She fit perfectly into the hollow of my arm. We stopped and kissed. It was so natural and beautiful, not jerky or tentative or rehearsed. I could feel her heart beating against me, and when we stopped, I noticed I'd forgotten about being in prison.

We spent the entire day talking and touching and looking. It was great. I wasn't nervous. As far as I know, I didn't say the wrong thing. We told each other everything from dreams to secrets, and when the sun began to set that night and the visiting room officer notified everyone that visiting was over, it seemed like she'd just arrived.

The next day was the same. Halfway through the afternoon, in the middle of a good, deep belly laugh, it dawned on me that this was the second day we'd ever been around one another, and here we were laughing like we'd grown up together; we'd been communicating for barely a month. It was a good sign.

"Can you believe this?" I asked her. I didn't have to explain what *this* was. She knew.

"I know," and then she smiled that smile and the sun came out.

As enjoyable as the weekend was, the opposite was true about the end of it and it was coming up on us too fast.

"I don't want to go back, Bo," she said.

"I know, baby. I know."

"Okay. Promise to tell me the truth?" she asked.

"You know I do," I said.

"Well, I want to know what you think about me moving to Oklahoma so I can be close to you and see you every weekend and get something started to help you get out."

The look on my face should've been answer enough, but she wanted to hear me say it.

"Well?"

"I, uh . . . " I was choked up, and fighting back tears. It was humbling enough having a perfectly normal young lady from an exceptionally good family give me her affection with no holds barred. Now here she was, wanting to change her whole life. I felt unworthy.

"I'd be the luckiest guy in the whole world, Deb.

That's what." I told her. I still tell her that.

She went back to Kentucky, but it was with the understanding she was coming back. Something I was to learn about Deb was that when she set her mind to something it was as good as done. Within two months she'd found a job and an apartment in Norman, a thirty-minute drive from the prison.

On a warm weekend in November, with the help of her parents, she loaded up her worldly belongings in her Chrysler and a U-Haul behind her dad's pickup, and they all headed to Oklahoma, mom and dad in tow. With a pink sign that said "BO OR BUST," they were on their way.

They made it out of Kentucky late. The fuel pump in Deb's car was shot. It was Friday night, and they were in a strange city. It had to be fate, though, because one merciful mechanic and a few hours later they were back on the road. They made it through Tennessee, Arkansas and into Oklahoma. I was about to meet mom and dad, and Deb was about to become an Okie.

That weekend was as beautiful as the weekend we'd met and sped by just as quickly. After meeting her parents, I better understood why I'd fallen in love with her. Good is an underrated and overused word, but there is no better word to describe Nick and Pat Rogers.

As it had happened with their daughter, I found myself feeling I'd known them all my life ten minutes after we'd met. They were as comfortable as a pair of overalls. I wanted to be a part of that family.

After the first weekend, Deb and I had discovered what we shared was special *and* serious. Call it true love. Call it youthful enthusiasm. Call it two lonely souls finding one another. Call it whatever you want, we started to discuss marriage.

I was not going to get married again while in prison. There was no discussion concerning that. I wasn't doing it; however, I knew I'd found the woman I wanted to be with, so we agreed on a long engagement. The way I saw it, it was an informal deal. It was between Deb and me.

Deb was from a family with old-fashioned morals; no man was *informally* engaged to their baby girl. I was going to have to ask dad for daughter's hand.

"I can't imagine what all this must be like for you, Nick." I began.

"Well, I'll tell ya." He rescued me from floundering. "I believe God knows what's best, and sometimes we might not see clearly, but it doesn't mean God is not right here. We raised Deb well, and we trust her judgment."

We spent the next few minutes talking about how special his youngest daughter was. He shared a couple of his favorite anecdotes. Then, as I was in the middle of telling him how much I loved Deb, and how much I wished I wasn't in prison, but I was, and I'd do anything for it not to be that way, he silenced me with a look.

"Bo?" he began. "All I ask is that you don't hurt her."

Nick was the most gentle man I'd ever met and yet there was no doubt in my mind he meant what he said with ice-cold gravity, a bottom line known only to dads who have daughters. I believed him.

Deb was now an official Okie. We saw each other

every weekend and talked on the phone every night, sent a daily letter apiece. That was one of the reasons she'd said she wanted to move to Oklahoma, and I agreed, it was a bargain for me. To this day, I've felt I was getting the better end of the deal.

A week didn't pass that we didn't talk about getting married and, although Deb said she understood my stand on the matter, I could tell she really didn't want to wait. We continued to talk about it, and I came to realize I couldn't continue not to take chances because I'd once made a mistake. It wasn't Deb's fault the person I had first married turned out to be someone who didn't know about truth or commitment. It wasn't Deb's fault I'd gotten married for the wrong reasons. None of the mistakes I'd made in my life were Deb's fault.

We compromised. On a gorgeous tailor-made November Sunday Deb and I sat on a picnic table and made some very serious vows to one another. We didn't invite a preacher, though Deb did consult her brother-in-law, Woody, on what necessities constitute a bona fide marriage.

With Woody's Southern Baptist-sanctioned contribution, the formal ceremony from an old worn-out Book of Common Prayer, and the words written on our hearts, we commenced pledging our lives to one another and to God. It was magical, and it was real. Looking into her green eyes, I never felt more right. Without documents or degrees, we were married, and it was good. God was smiling on us.

"Well? Is that it?" I asked when we'd gotten to the point where I was pretty sure we were finished with everything but the kissing part.

"Yeah, I guess so," Deb smiled back. I was reminded of a scene from *The Adventures of Huckleberry Finn* where young Tom Sawyer and Becky Thatcher pledged eternal love for one another. He'd given her his favorite marble or a doorknob or something of equal value, and she'd given him her ribbon, I think. Suddenly, it was time to kiss, although neither of them had ever done it before. Even though Deb and I were twenty-five and thirty-four, our love felt as young and unspoiled as the love I remember feeling the first time I read that scene.

We kissed to seal the deal.

"Look," she said. It was barely a whisper. She was looking up into the sky. I followed her gaze. There wasn't a cloud to be seen. At first, I thought she was just pointing out the beauty of that clear sky. Then I saw them. Two hawks circling lazily overhead.

"Wow," I said. It was a nice touch to a beautiful day and a very special moment.

If it never got any better, I'd count myself fortunate, but it has. We grow more and more in love every day, as I learn more about this woman I'm so blessed to call my wife and friend.

Holding down a forty-hour-per-week-job, writing me every night, she also spends many hours on the road or at prison. Between that and the countless other things that constitute her life—including regular, tiring, painful bouts with endometriosis—she's raised enough money to hire the best appellate lawyer in the state. She's gearing up a concerted effort at parole. She won't quit. I'm not saying she won't get tired. I'm sure she will. When she does, one of my jobs will be to help her learn to slow down, take a break and refuel.

My head swims when I sit down and comprehend all that she is. I don't know what I did to deserve her. When I'd given up on love, God put a person in my life who *is* love. I didn't choose her. She chose me. She tells people she ordered me out of a catalog.

It's not a traditional love story, indicative of some of the lessons God has taught me. "Don't try to control me, son, just let me run this thing called creation. I'm much better suited at it, and you'll be more pleased with what I give you than with anything you could have done on your own. Sit back and do your best. Don't worry if you mess up, because I'm a master at turning those situations into wonderful and unfathomable blessings."

In case you are wondering when we're going to get "legally" married, don't worry. Not long after I was transferred to another prison, we had a simple and holy ceremony, complete with marriage license, parents, and a preacher. The prison officials wouldn't allow photographs, but no picture could do justice to the memory I keep in my heart.

Last weekend, my wife and I talked about the day she saw my picture in a magazine.

"I sure am glad I ordered you," she giggled.

Me too, Deb. Me too.

Colorado

For where two or three come together in my name, there I am with them. —Matthew 18:20

I called my Dad this morning. He's retired now, and it's possible for us to have early morning conversations. It's the next best thing to drinking a cup of coffee with my father. It's fresh, a chance for us to be who we really are before we are heated and hammered on the forges of everyday life. This morning at about seven-thirty a really wonderful thing happened.

Dad had spent the previous week in Colorado, up in the mountains, horseback riding. He and a few of his friends had loaded the horses, hitched the trailers and made the trek. He'd been talking about it for months. Last year was his first year to go, and I can remember his tone of voice when he returned. Something special was up in those mountains, and he'd found it. For a year now he'd been telling me that when I got out he and I were going. Earlier in the year when a court case that directly affected my sentence had been overturned, we thought there was a possibility that I might even be out in time to make this year's trip. Obviously, it didn't happen, and Dad had spent the last few months assuring me that it was still in our destiny.

I believed that. I don't really know on what level, but I knew that, yes, someday I'd be in the mountains with him. I had my own belief in the holy beauty of creation in it's raw, unblemished splendor and, coupled with Dad's tales of last year's trip, I knew it'd be a spiritual experience, but I had no idea how absolutely miraculous that realization would turn out to be.

"Well, Colorado man, how'd it go?" I asked when he picked up the phone.

"Oh, son, it was unbelievably special." He began telling me who had made the ride with him. They were all people from my hometown, people I'd known since childhood. But, as had become custom over the last few years, he'd have to remind me how I knew these used-to-be-familiar names. Who had been married to whom and where they lived, whose son was whose and how he was six foot tall, when the boy I remembered was still in grade school. It always makes me sad when I realize how much I've forgotten about the world where I used to live.

"As we drove up, we went through a herd of elk. Must've been two, three hundred."

I was looking through one of the large windows that encompass our dayroom, out at other prisoners starting their week. Men were going to work, coming back from breakfast, sitting around drinking coffee, rolling and smoking cigarettes on our small unit yard. Just another Monday morning in prison.

I wasn't conscious when it happened, but suddenly I was seeing a herd of elk. They were leisurely strolling

through a huge valley in the middle of magnificent mountains. Above them, in the clear blue sky, soared an eagle; however, it seemed like the very instant I became aware of it, the elk turned back into blue-shirted men, the eagle was a starling, and I was back on the phone with Dad.

He was describing the third or fourth morning. A couple of the men his age had gone off to fish, and he was sitting around with a couple of the young men I remember as little league players.

"By the way, son, Mark said to tell you that he thinks about you a lot."

It touched me that this kid even remembered me, much less wondered how I was doing. Again, for a brief flash, I was sitting at the campfire with them. I had a tin coffee cup, full of steaming strong, black coffee that I could smell along with the smoke from the neatly-burning fire and, again, I didn't notice the plastic phone in my hand or the hum of the exhaust fans as they pulled the cigarette smoke and smell of caged men out through the ceiling. Dad's voice pulled me back.

"Anyway, I want to tell you something. I started a prayer, actually it's a chant, for you while I was up there. I walked out in the woods, and it came to me I'd been going out daily by myself and talking to the Creator. We had some good talks. As a matter of fact, we're not through. I'm going back this weekend. The point is, the fellas were used to me walking off into the woods and knew what I was doing. So, like I said, we were sitting around the fire and I told Mark I had to go do my thing and he said, 'Go take care of it.'"

Dad's voice was getting strained. Love or pain were near the surface.

"I was out there on a ridge, and God and I were talking, and I began your chant," he continued. I was wondering what it was, this chant he was speaking of. He continued:

"Set him free."

He described the scene, the trees, the wind, but I wasn't listening. There was a huge lump in my throat.

Even if I'd wanted to, I couldn't have spoken. I could feel the wind on that Colorado mountain blowing through my body. I could smell the pines and for the tiniest, and yet most eternal, moment I was in that prayer. I could see my dad standing in the morning sun, lifting his grizzled gray beard and blue eyes into the wind, lifting up all that he had, including his son, to our Creator.

For just an instant I could feel the pain my father has having with his son being in prison and not being able to do one thing to get him out. I didn't feel guilty or sorry for Dad. I just felt.

I struggled to find my voice, to stop the overwhelming flow of every feeling I'd ever had coursing through me. I had to tell this man, this father of mine, how much I loved him.

"Dad," I blurted out, "I love you."

"Oh, Bo, I love you, too." Through tears he managed to say he believed everything was going to be all right.

"I know, Dad, I know."

As I hung up the phone, I realized I'd forgotten to tell him something: his prayer has been answered.

Grandpa

Stubbornly they turned their backs on you, became stiff necked and refused to listen. For many years you were patient with them. —Nehemiah 9:29, 30

"Cox, 150656, you've got a visit!" the day-shift guard barked from the dayroom, snatching me away from my clean-air, wide-open daydream and thrusting me back into my cinder block and cement world. I hadn't been expecting anyone, and I wondered who had come to see me.

I reached under my bunk to grab my boots and as I looked them over, trying to decide whether to brush them, my mind drifted to my boots' previous owner, Eddie Don Cox. My grandpa.

The noon sun was baking a hillside littered with discarded refrigerators-turned-storage bins and car-hoods-turned-feed troughs. In the distance sat an old skeleton of a building that had once been the town's lumber company. Sitting up on blocks like a junk car, it was on its way to becoming a barn. Rusty barbed wire strung on twisted posts dissected the scrub oak and sandstone landscape.

Grandpa, the artist of this picture, the director of the show, the man who had put this all together, was sitting on a feed trough built out of used sheet iron and railroad ties. He took his crumpled, sweat-stained straw cowboy hat off his head and wiped his forehead with his sleeve. Then he smiled his crooked smile and his eyes sparkled from between the hard-earned wrinkles.

"Shore is hot, ain't it, boy?" We'd spent the morning laying rock, building a fireplace and chimney on the side of a dirty white frame house he'd moved from town. It was mostly unspoken, but the truth was, that old house was slated to be my home. Only thing was, I didn't want a home. More accurately, I didn't want the responsibility. At that time in my life I was content to live in town with my mom and spend the $5 per hour I earned from Grandpa, and anyone else who'd put up with my erratic work habits, on drugs. That, sadly, was the sum of my existence.

"Yes sir, it is that." I was imagining how good an iced-down beer would taste, or better yet, a couple of good joints and a six pack on the bank of a swimming hole.

"You know, son, you need to quit that drinking." As usual, he had read my mind.

"Yeah, I know. I'm gonna cut down. Hell, though, I really don't drink as much as you think I do." I lied.

He let it go and shook his head. I grinned at him. We were as close as two people so separated by generations could be. Even though I knew we had a special relationship, it's too bad I didn't know how special. His unconditional love went over my head.

A few years later, that love was a raging, blazing

fire in those blue eyes as it sought to communicate the full range of emotions contained within Grandpa. I was in the county jail and this time it wasn't for public drunkeness, possession of paraphernalia, or an open container. The night before, drunk as usual, I'd killed another young man in a fight. I can only assume it must've been the most difficult thing to do, yet there he was, standing tall beside me, letting the whole world know that we were the same two partners that had built that somewhat lopsided chimney together.

Later, after I was convicted and sent to prison, he continued to stand beside me. Grandpa had a hard time sitting still, but there he'd be, fidgeting around in the crowded prison visiting room, looking around at the assortment of human beings contained there.

"It takes all kinds, don't it boy?" he'd invariably ask.

"Sure does, Grandpa."

"You oughtta try AA, son. Do they have it here?"

"Yeah, uh, I've gone a couple of times. It's all right." Truth was, I hadn't ever sat foot inside an AA meeting. I was still going full steam ahead with my addictions and had no time for AA, church, or anything else that threatened the chemical safety net I had wrapped around my world.

As he'd been doing for longer than I now care to remember, he once again shook his head and dropped the subject. But not without smiling that crooked smile at me, as if to let me know that even though I was full of it, he loved me anyway.

Prison visiting rooms are loud and stressful, and it wouldn't take long for him to get restless. He'd stay long enough to assure himself that I was at least getting by and then he'd unfold his six-two frame from the plastic chair and stand up.

"You've got yourself in a helluva mess this time, boy." He'd grin that grin, as if to say he was in it with me. Then he'd shake my hand and walk out the door, never looking back.

Even though he knew I still hadn't changed my habits, he couldn't stand the fact I was in prison. I hadn't been in long when, one night on the phone, Dad told me that all grandpa had been talking about lately was getting me out of prison. "Son, you just don't know. He can't stand you being there. It's eating him up," Dad said. "All he's been saying is 'Gotta get that boy outta there.'"

Through others, I learned that had become his credo.

After I had been in prison about three years, a guard came to my cell and told me I had an emergency phone call. As I picked up the phone, I feared what I was about to hear. Dad confirmed it.

The next day I was granted an emergency visit to see Grandpa. I'll never, as long as I live, forget the smile Grandpa managed when he opened his tired old eyes and saw me standing there, chained and shackled. It was that same ol' crooked grin. It spoke volumes and it almost brought me to my knees.

I spent the next hour-and-a-half standing next to his bed, holding his hand and looking into his eyes. Not a word was spoken. He couldn't talk, and I was afraid to open my mouth for fear of breaking down and losing the tiny grasp I had on my emotions. In a small gesture of mimicking the unconditional love he'd always shown toward me, I didn't once let go of his hand, even though my hands went to sleep because of the handcuffs.

The only thing I'd seen for those ninety minutes were Grandpa's eyes and the tops of my shoes. His eyes had me. At the time, I couldn't comprehend all they contained. He was saying something with them, but I wasn't ready to hear. Every few seconds it'd become too intense for me and I'd look away, down at the tops of my feet. Then I'd look back up. There was simply too much for me to handle at that point in my life.

Then again, maybe not. On the way back to prison I said an earnest prayer, perhaps the first in many years, for Grandpa. And, then, I said one for myself.

Eventually, he recovered. Gradually, he even became strong enough to make trips up to see me. He looked tired, but also looked determined. He still got restless after a short time, but that was understandable. This place did make you want to go home.

He got better and began again telling people, "Gotta get that boy outta there." Dad said he thought it was giving him an extra little something to live for.

It was not enough. Grandpa, the best friend I never knew I had, died September 22, 1989.

I was allowed to attend the funeral. I'd been up two or three days, shooting amphetamines and was a walking mess when the day came. All I remember was feeling self-conscious as I stood in the church with my chains and shackles. The chains seemed unusually loud when they unlocked one hand so I could help my brother and five cousins, the grandsons, carry him to his grave. It felt like everyone was looking at me, and my shame was a lot heavier than the hardware surrounding me.

Still, I hope I stood as tall beside him as he'd always stood beside me.

"Cox! The visiting room just called. Your visit's waiting for you," another khaki-clad officer yelled up at me. I was still sitting there with one boot in my hands, absentmindedly running my fingers over the ripples of the shark's long dead skin and wondering how long they'd last before I wore them out.

I decided right then I was going to take good enough care of them to wear them when I got out.

* * *

This was originally written and published in *Concepts* in 1994. I still haven't gotten out of prison. But less than a year after Grandpa died I managed to achieve the sobriety he so longed for me to have. Sometimes I dream about my grandpa and, when I do, he's still got that crooked grin. And I think today he's proud of me and that feels good.

If you don't have a Grandpa, take part of mine. He's too special not to share.

If you do, take a minute to look into his eyes and tell him how much you love him. You don't have to say a word.

God Is Not In
the Thesaurus

Blessed are the poor in spirit . . . Blessed are those who mourn . . . Blessed are the meek . . . Blessed are those who hunger and thirst for righteousness . . . Blessed are the merciful . . . Blessed are the pure in heart . . . Blessed are the peacemakers . . . Blessed are those who are persecuted because of righteousness . . .
—Matthew 5:3-10

What a ragged lot. Who wants to be poor-spirited? Who wants to mourn? Who wants to be meek? Hungering and thirsting for righteousness leaves me hungry and thirsty. Being merciful and pure in heart is too close to perfect—who wants to be a goody-two-shoes? Peacemaker? If it's not too much trouble. Being persecuted for righteousness is downright unfair. Martyrdom isn't all it's cracked up to be.

It puzzles me then that Jesus would say that if we are any of these, we'll have the kingdom of heaven, be comforted, inherit the earth, be filled, shown mercy, see

God, be called children of God. I suppose it must be some more of that "less is more," "no pain, no gain," philosophy that seems prevalent in the Bible. It appears that pain *is* the touchstone of spiritual growth.

I don't like pain. Never have. My first instinct is to run away from it. That's one of the reasons drugs appealed to me so much. I was fifteen years old the first time I got loaded. It was during a very turbulent period in my life, when I was changing, becoming a man, and thought I was the only kid in the world so confused and so scared that I never knew what to do. The most important thing in the world to me was that people never know how scared and unsure I was. When you're fifteen (and sometimes when you're thirty-five) the only thing that matters is being cool and having everyone think you're cool. Deep down, though, I knew I was anything but cool.

I remember the first time. After two joints and four beers, I was watching the smoke curl off the tip of a cigarette, amazed at how good I felt. No fear. No pain. I felt good. If you'd told me that Jesus said suffering produced supernatural results I would have giggled and said that good weed and cold beer do it faster. I thought I had found *the* answer. Unfortunately for me and countless others, drugs and alcohol do a more than adequate job of killing pain and masking fear—just for a while. Then they add to your fear and your pain, and more alcohol and drugs are needed. It's an endless, self-feeding, vicious cycle. Millions of people know all about it.

Too many of us end up in jails and prisons. Others end up in hospitals, institutions, treatment centers. Some of us finally find peace in cemeteries. While most of us may never set foot inside any sort of institution, we know pain. To be human is to know pain.

But alcoholics and addicts don't have a corner on the pain market. If your heart beats, you've hurt. All of us—bankers, convicts, construction workers, prisoners, priests, three-time losers, doctors, lawyers, treatment center dropouts, middle school students, patients, republicans, clients, democrats, drunks, college students, junkies, professors, losers, winners, housewives, homeless people, CEOs, janitors, taxpayers, welfare recipients, working stiffs, wards of the state, mothers, fathers, factory workers, accountants, children, nursing home residents, death row inmates, church deacons, victims, victimizers, and everyone else who has ever suffered—are connected.

This book is for all connected people, all children of God, all of us.

Blessed and suffering, I live in a prison. I've been here for thirteen years. I've seen the meek, poor in spirit, and humble people. I've seen God in these folks. After you have read these stories, I hope you've seen God in someone you know, even in yourself. God *is* around, and maybe not where you expect.

Not long ago, writing a poem, I wanted a synonym for the word, God. I highlighted *God* and moved my cursor to the thesaurus icon at the top of the screen and clicked.

God is not in the thesaurus, it said.

What? How could God, the omniscient, the omnipotent, the omnipresent, not be in the thesaurus? God should be everywhere. I chuckled at the computer's deficiency and began to get the mental image of God who is everywhere—even in lap-top computers, even in prison. How many times and in how many places and in how many ways has God been here?

How was it possible that had I lived for so many years believing that God was only to be found in heaven or in church? Until I was sent to prison, I never would have guessed that God lived here—where murderers, thieves, rapists, child molesters, drug dealers and robbers live. Among society's outcasts, I have found God. Or, more accurately—because an old friend has said, "God wasn't lost, you were"—it was God who found me.

It shouldn't be surprising. God is in here. Jesus would have loved prison. Were Jesus walking around today, what would people think about a son of God who spent a substantial amount of his time in prisons? Visiting the very people that society has exiled—people in crack houses, shooting galleries, parks with the homeless, mental institutions, homes for unwed mothers, slums?

I can see it all now. The pastor of a big downtown church is in the pulpit before a huge stained-glass window. Enormous building, weekly radio broadcast, heavenly choir, social outreach programs, successful business people, community leaders. Perfect. Sunday morning. Everyone in suits and dresses. Lunch after the service. Today's big surprise: Jesus is going to be here and tell the church what it *really* means to be Christian.

"Ahem," the pastor clears his throat. "As you all know, Jeeezzzuss, was scheduled to be here today. You were going to hear from the Lord himself the ABCs of Christianity, how to be Christ-like. However, this morning we received a call to say he'll be at the state prison, passing up a chance to dine on our fine potluck dinner, so he can eat one of those jail lunches with the very same sinners who have committed atrocious crimes. I'm so sorry. I know it's a disappointment."

Outside of town at the prison, in the dark chow hall, things are not that much different. All week long, Johny, the long-haired man with the bright eyes, who everyone thinks is a little crazy, has been telling his fellow prisoners that Jesus is coming to eat lunch with them on Sunday. No one believed him.

"Nah, you're crazy Johny," they all said. "Jesus is for the good people, people who do right. We've lost our chance. Didn't you ever pay attention in church?"

"I'm telling you guys, he's coming to eat with us. He wants to hang out with us, too," Johny insisted.

No one believed him.

At lunch all the prisoners are sitting at their long tables, heads bowed, shoveling bland prison food down their throats as fast as possible. All you hear is the scrape of plastic spoon against plastic tray, the jingle of the guard's keys and an occasional grunt.

"Excuse me. Could I join you guys? Maybe break a little bread? I've got some really good news, if you want to hear it."

Johny's not crazy and that's why I wrote this book.

Jeff Weimar provides the illustrations used throughout the book. A friend of the author's, he, too is an inmate in the Oklahoma correctional system. In addition to painting, Mr. Weimar writes poetry, sculpts, and is a devotee of herbal healing. He is an avid runner.

Richard Martin created the front cover illustration. He has a flair for the potter's wheel, as well as painting. He is planning a gallery of water-colors for the internet. He, too, is a friend and fellow inmate of Bo Cox.

**Other publications
by Bo Don Cox
from
Forward Movement Publications**

The Impact of Divorce

Release

Silent Night